This guide is made possible

by the support of Genentech BioOncology

BIO**2**NCOLOGY™

Genentech
A Member of the Roche Group

cure's
Illustrated
Guide
to Cancer

cure's Illustrated Guide to Cancer

curemedia**group**

Dallas, Texas

Published by
CURE Media Group
3102 Oak Lawn Avenue, Suite 610
Dallas, Texas 75219
www.curetoday.com

Information presented is not intended as a substitute for the personalized professional advice given by your health care provider. The publishers urge readers to contact appropriately qualified health professionals for advice on any health or lifestyle change inspired by information herein.

This publication was produced by CURE Media Group through the financial support of Genentech. The views expressed in this publication are not necessarily those of Genentech or the publishers. Although great care has been taken to ensure accuracy, CURE Media Group and its servants or agents shall not be responsible or in any way liable for the continued currency of the information or for any errors, omissions, or inaccuracies in this book, whether arising from negligence or otherwise or for any consequences arising there from. Parts of this book were first published in *CURE* magazine and are reprinted here in slightly different form. Review and creation of content is solely the responsibility of CURE Media Group. CURE Media Group is affiliated with US Oncology, Inc., the nation's leading oncology services company expanding patient access to advanced cancer care.

Any mention of retail products does not constitute an endorsement by the authors or the publisher.

Library of Congress Control Number: 2010903080

ISBN 978-0-980130843

Editors: Lena Huang and Debu Tripathy, MD
Design: Susan Douglass
Layout: Glenn Zamora
Medical illustrations: Lewis E. Calver; Pam Curry, Physicians' Education Resource; Erin Moore, Physicians' Education Resource; and Jim Perkins
Scientific advisor: Diane Gambill, PhD, Physicians' Education Resource

Printed in the United States of America

Table *of* Contents

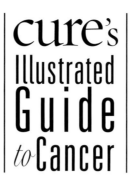

Introduction

THE OLD ADAGE that a picture is worth a thousand words could not be more appropriate when it comes to understanding cancer. From the origins of cancer and to how it is diagnosed and treated to where the future will take us, we have been impressed by the power of illustration. Our readers, including patients, friends and family, and cancer care professionals, have all referenced our drawings as an effective communication tool that enriches the message—making it easier to retain and digest, no matter how complicated and convoluted the subject matter.

We compiled our most informative and relevant illustrations, judged by our own staff and readers. We also used pictures that nurses and physicians have cited as particularly helpful in explaining the cancer types, how it is affecting the body, how it will be treated, and what to expect from the cancer journey. We discussed the drawings as a team over multiple meetings, phone calls, and e-mails, then enhanced them to provide both the accuracy and detail that characterizes human biology as well as the intuitive sense of relevance to demonstrate why it is important to the individual with cancer. *CURE's Illustrated Guide to Cancer* is an atlas, a map, a storybook, designed to empower you in the best way—with knowledge.

Debu Tripathy, MD
Editor-in-chief, *CURE*

CURE's Illustrated Guide to Cancer

Chapter 1

About Cancer

CANCER ORIGINATES from the uncontrolled growth of abnormal cells. In the body, normal cells follow a pattern of growth, division, and death. However, cancer cells follow their own pattern—growing, dividing, and forming more abnormal cells. This growth may occur in adjacent cells, or cancerous cells may travel to distant locations in the body through the blood or lymphatic systems, which is called metastasis. There are many types of cancer, and cancer cells can develop in different parts of the body. Some cancer cells form solid tumors while others involve the blood or bone marrow. Cancer strikes people of all ages, although the risk of many cancers increases with age.

Tumor Environment

[
The complex environment in which a tumor thrives plays a role
in cancer growth and metastasis.
]

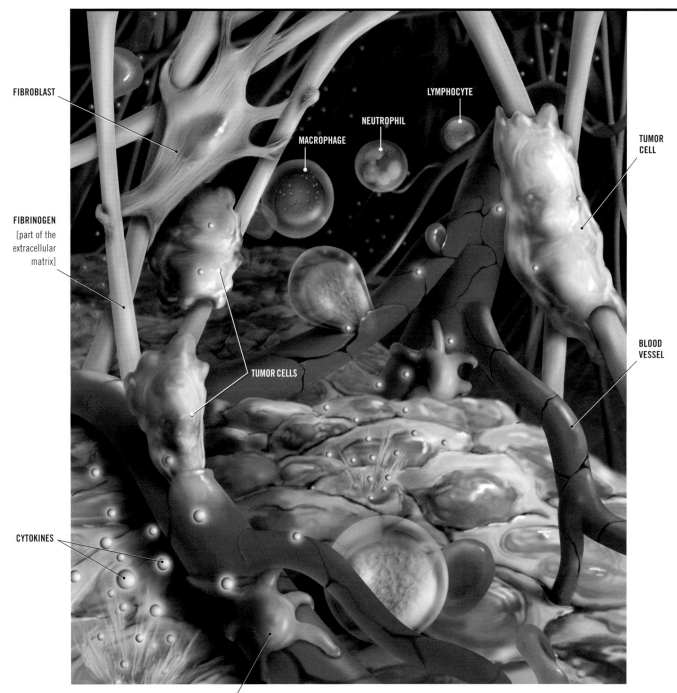

FIBROBLAST

FIBRINOGEN
[part of the
extracellular
matrix]

CYTOKINES

PERICYTE

MACROPHAGE

NEUTROPHIL

LYMPHOCYTE

TUMOR CELLS

TUMOR
CELL

BLOOD
VESSEL

ELEMENTS IN THE TUMOR ENVIRONMENT >

BLOOD VESSELS that nourish the tumor are "leaky" and have other differences compared with normal blood vessels. They are, therefore, the target of some current cancer-fighting drugs in a class known as antiangiogenics.

Pro-inflammatory **CYTOKINES,** immune system–signaling molecules that contribute to inflammation, can promote tumor blood vessel growth, sustain viability of dangerous precancerous cells, and prompt some cells to reproduce faster, increasing their risk of mutation.

NEUTROPHILS and **LYMPHOCYTES** are immune system cells that can tip the balance toward a cancer-promoting or cancer-inhibiting microenvironment. An abundance of neutrophils is associated with increased growth of tumor blood vessels and a poor prognosis. High levels of lymphocytes have been linked to a better prognosis.

FIBRINOGEN, which normally plays a role in clot formation, may indirectly affect tumor growth, metastasis, and blood vessel formation.

TUMOR CELLS; cancer-associated fibroblasts; immune system components known as tumor-associated **MACROPHAGES;** and **PERICYTES,** cells adjacent to the tumor blood vessel lining, release enzymes that alter the structure of the extracellular matrix. Remodeling the matrix—the scaffolding of tissue that supports cells—makes it easier for tumors to invade and spread.

Cause & Effect

[Cancer can be caused by environmental factors, random events, or hereditary factors.]

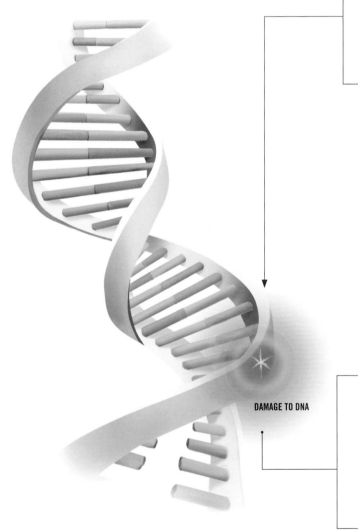

DAMAGE TO DNA

SPORADIC CANCERS

The majority of cancer diagnoses are considered sporadic. These tumors are the result of **environmental exposures** or possible **random events** within a cell.

HEREDITARY CANCERS

Hereditary cancers result from an **inherited gene mutation or variation** that is present in every cell and can be passed on to children. **Familial cancer** refers to hereditary cancers that may be due to shared environmental or lifestyle factors.

SOLID TUMORS

An abnormal mass of tissue, solid tumors are named for the type of cells that form them. Examples are sarcomas and carcinomas.

LIQUID TUMORS

Cancers of the blood, such as leukemias, are sometimes referred to as liquid tumors.

ABOUT CANCER

1

ILLUSTRATION BY PAM CURRY

Metastasis

Cancer cells may travel to distant parts of the body through the blood or lymphatic system, which is called metastasis.

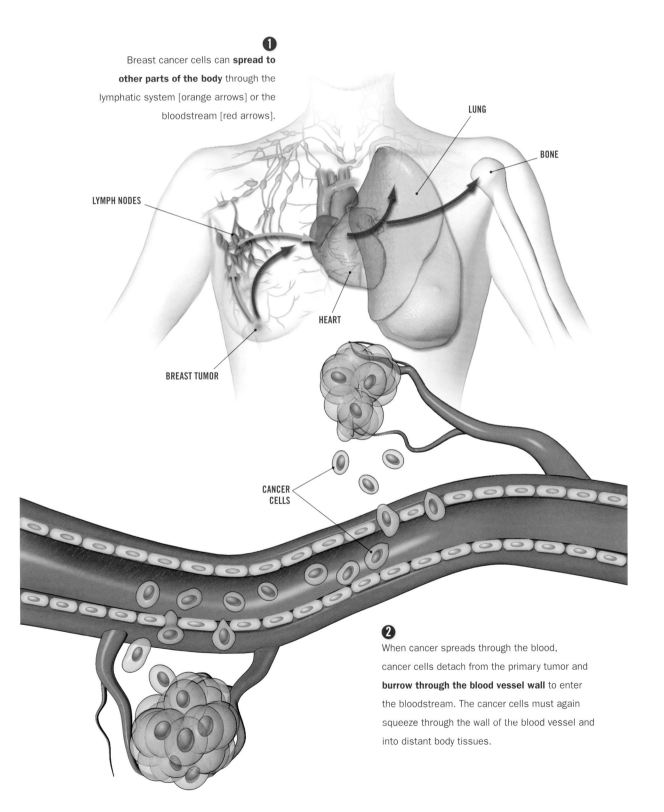

❶ Breast cancer cells can **spread to other parts of the body** through the lymphatic system [orange arrows] or the bloodstream [red arrows].

LUNG

BONE

LYMPH NODES

HEART

BREAST TUMOR

CANCER CELLS

❷ When cancer spreads through the blood, cancer cells detach from the primary tumor and **burrow through the blood vessel wall** to enter the bloodstream. The cancer cells must again squeeze through the wall of the blood vessel and into distant body tissues.

ILLUSTRATION BY ERIN MOORE

cure's
Illustrated
Guide
to Cancer

Chapter 2

Cancer Staging

STAGING, an integral part of the cancer diagnosis, helps physicians determine the patient's

treatment plan and prognosis. It also provides nurses, health care providers, doctors, and

researchers a common language to discuss a patient's cancer. Staging describes the extent

of the cancer. For most cancers, it is based on location of the primary tumor, size of the

tumor, how many tumors are present, and whether the cancer has spread to nearby organs,

tissues, lymph nodes, or distant parts of the body. TNM staging is the most commonly used

system and is based on T, the primary tumor or place where the cancer began; N, the level of

lymph node involvement; and M, the presence or absence of metastasis.

Cancer Staging

Staging defines how much cancer exists and whether the cancer has spread to other parts of the body. General staging information varies for specific kinds of cancer.

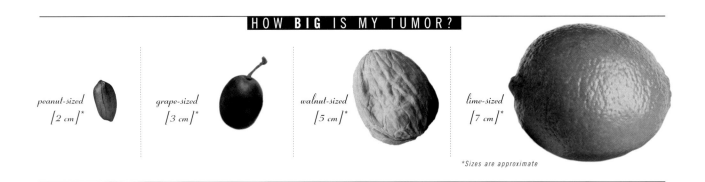

HOW **BIG** IS MY TUMOR?

peanut-sized
[2 cm]*

grape-sized
[3 cm]*

walnut-sized
[5 cm]*

lime-sized
[7 cm]*

*Sizes are approximate

Typical TNM Tumor Staging System

Primary Tumor (T)	
TX	Primary tumor cannot be evaluated
T0	No evidence of primary tumor
Tis	Carcinoma in situ
T1, T2, T3, T4	Depends on size and/or extent of primary tumor
Regional Lymph Nodes (N)	
NX	Regional lymph nodes cannot be evaluated
N0	No regional lymph node involvement
N1, N2, N3	Depends on number/extent of spread to regional lymph nodes
Distant Metastasis (M)	
MX	Distant metastasis cannot be evaluated
M0	Cancer has not spread to other parts of the body
M1	Cancer has spread to other parts of the body

Overall Stage Groupings

STAGE	DESCRIPTION
Stage 0	Carcinoma in situ
Stage 1 to 3	More extensive disease indicated by higher numbers (could include larger tumor, cancer present in nearby lymph nodes, and/or cancer present in organs adjacent to the organ in which the cancer began)
Stage 4	Cancer has spread to a distant organ

Noninvasive Breast Cancer

Screening and management recommendations are detailed for each cellular change of noninvasive breast cancer.

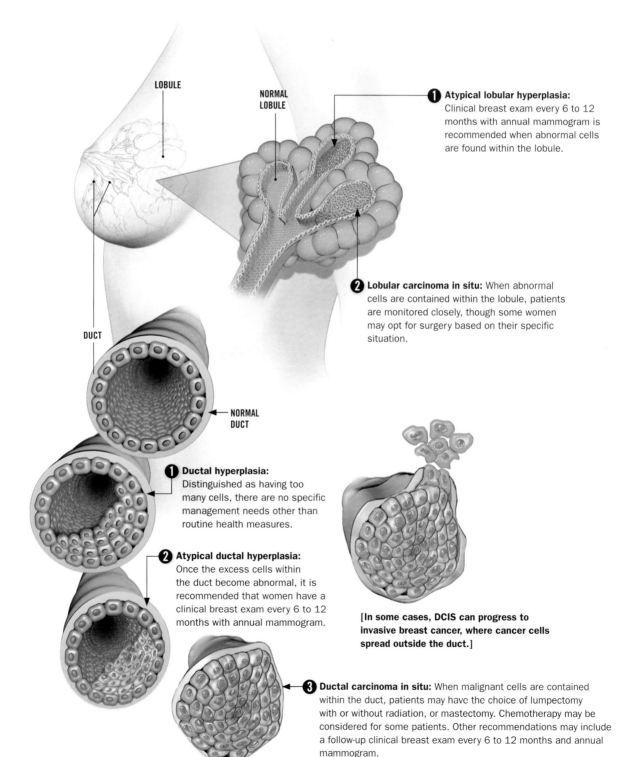

LOBULE

NORMAL LOBULE

① Atypical lobular hyperplasia: Clinical breast exam every 6 to 12 months with annual mammogram is recommended when abnormal cells are found within the lobule.

② Lobular carcinoma in situ: When abnormal cells are contained within the lobule, patients are monitored closely, though some women may opt for surgery based on their specific situation.

DUCT

NORMAL DUCT

① Ductal hyperplasia: Distinguished as having too many cells, there are no specific management needs other than routine health measures.

② Atypical ductal hyperplasia: Once the excess cells within the duct become abnormal, it is recommended that women have a clinical breast exam every 6 to 12 months with annual mammogram.

[In some cases, DCIS can progress to invasive breast cancer, where cancer cells spread outside the duct.]

③ Ductal carcinoma in situ: When malignant cells are contained within the duct, patients may have the choice of lumpectomy with or without radiation, or mastectomy. Chemotherapy may be considered for some patients. Other recommendations may include a follow-up clinical breast exam every 6 to 12 months and annual mammogram.

ILLUSTRATION BY ERIN MOORE
SOURCE: *ANNALS OF INTERNAL MEDICINE*; *CURE* RESEARCH

Invasive Breast Cancer

The American Joint Committee on Cancer's TNM staging system is the standard system used to classify breast cancer.

The TNM staging system is based on T, for tumor; N, for spread to the lymph nodes; and M, for metastasis (spread to distant tissues or organs). Additional letters or numbers, which provide more details of the tumor, lymph nodes, or metastasis, may follow the TNM stages.

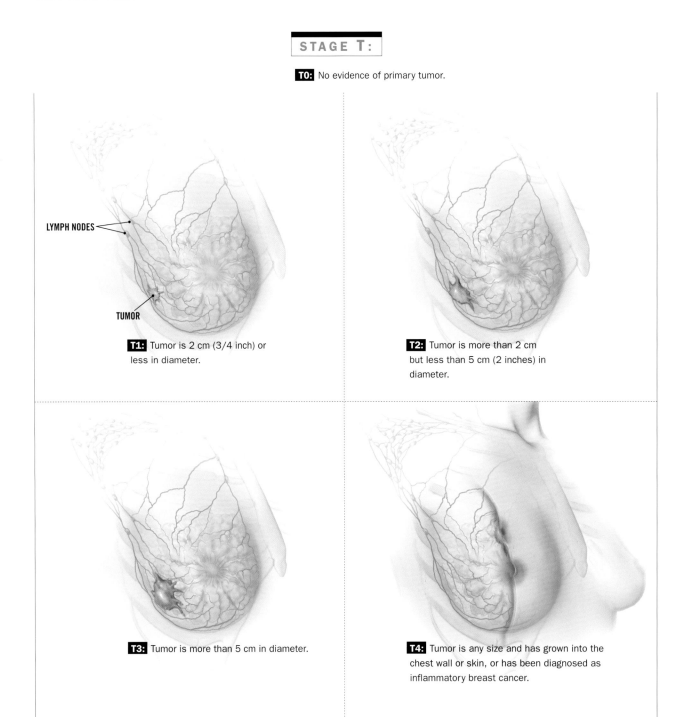

STAGE T:

T0: No evidence of primary tumor.

LYMPH NODES

TUMOR

T1: Tumor is 2 cm (3/4 inch) or less in diameter.

T2: Tumor is more than 2 cm but less than 5 cm (2 inches) in diameter.

T3: Tumor is more than 5 cm in diameter.

T4: Tumor is any size and has grown into the chest wall or skin, or has been diagnosed as inflammatory breast cancer.

CANCER STAGING

2

STAGE N:

N0: Cancer has not spread to nearby lymph nodes.

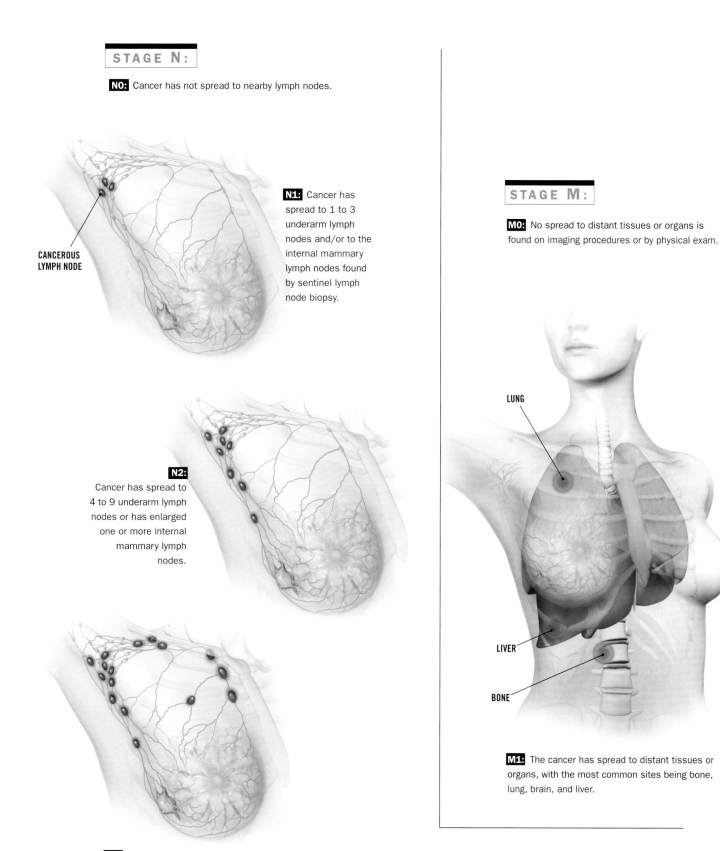

CANCEROUS
LYMPH NODE

N1: Cancer has spread to 1 to 3 underarm lymph nodes and/or to the internal mammary lymph nodes found by sentinel lymph node biopsy.

N2: Cancer has spread to 4 to 9 underarm lymph nodes or has enlarged one or more internal mammary lymph nodes.

STAGE M:

M0: No spread to distant tissues or organs is found on imaging procedures or by physical exam.

LUNG

LIVER

BONE

M1: The cancer has spread to distant tissues or organs, with the most common sites being bone, lung, brain, and liver.

N3: Described as one of the following:

■ Cancer has spread to 10 or more underarm lymph nodes with at least one area measuring more than 2 mm. (N3a)

■ Cancer has spread to the lymph nodes under the collarbone with at least one area measuring more than 2 mm. (N3a)

■ Cancer has spread to 1 or more underarm lymph nodes with at least one area measuring more than 2 mm, and has enlarged one or more internal mammary lymph nodes. (N3b)

■ Cancer has spread to 4 or more underarm lymph nodes with at least one area measuring more than 2 mm, and to the internal mammary lymph nodes found by sentinel lymph node biopsy. (N3b)

■ Cancer has spread to the lymph nodes above the collarbone with at least one area measuring more than 2 mm. (N3c)

Prostate Cancer

When diagnosing prostate cancer, doctors consider staging and grading. In grading, a score is assigned based on the Gleason grading system.

Stage 1:

The cancer is located on one side of the prostate. At this stage, the tumor is very small or found accidentally, possibly during surgery or by an elevated prostate-specific antigen (PSA) level. The Gleason score is low.

Stage 2:

The cancer is located only in the prostate but can be seen on imaging scans or felt during a digital rectal exam. The Gleason score may range from 2 to 10.

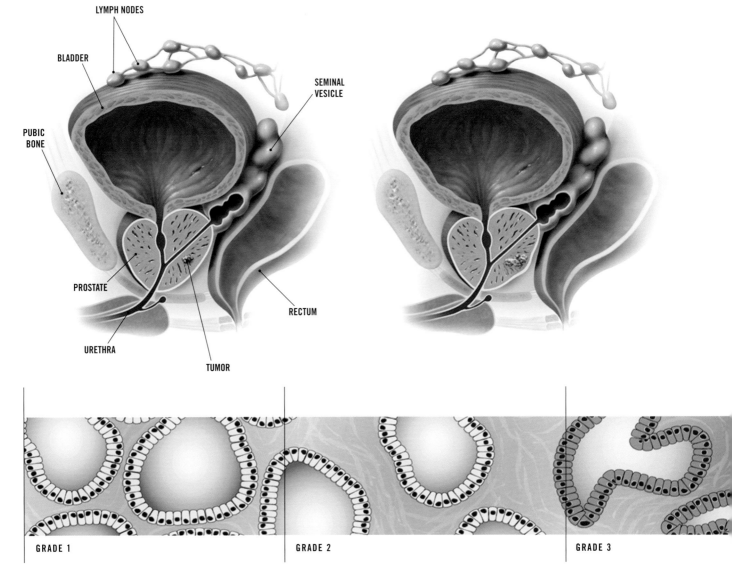

LYMPH NODES

BLADDER

SEMINAL VESICLE

PUBIC BONE

PROSTATE

RECTUM

URETHRA

TUMOR

GRADE 1

GRADE 2

GRADE 3

The Gleason grading system defines prostate cancer by grade based on the pathologist's review of a biopsy or surgical specimen, with 1 being the least aggressive and 5 being the most aggressive. The grade of the most common tumor pattern is added to the grade of the second most common tumor pattern in the tissue examined to create the Gleason score. A Gleason score of 2 to 4 is considered low grade, 5 to 7 is intermediate grade, and 8 to 10 is high grade.

2 CANCER STAGING

Stage 3:

The cancer has extended through the outer layer of the prostate and into surrounding tissues and may be found in the seminal vesicle but not in the lymph nodes. The Gleason score may range from 2 to 10.

Stage 4:

The cancer has spread to the lymph nodes near or far from the prostate or has spread to distant tissue or organs, such as the liver or bones. The Gleason score may range from 2 to 10.

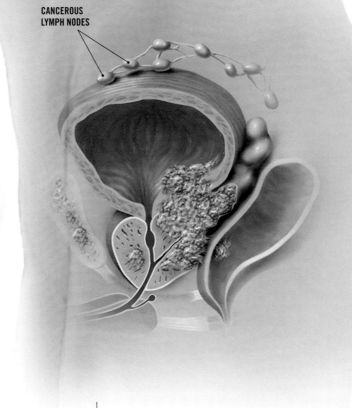

CANCEROUS
LYMPH NODES

GRADE 4

GRADE 5

Non-Small Cell Lung Cancer

Following a lung cancer diagnosis, staging determines the best options for treatment.
Many factors are evaluated, including the size of the tumor and the extent of spread.

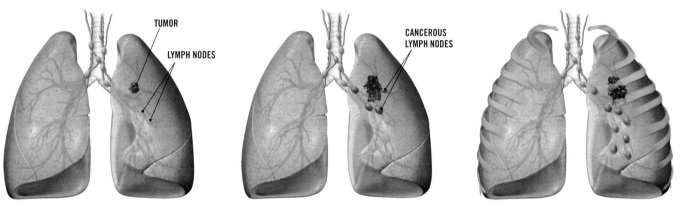

TUMOR

LYMPH NODES

CANCEROUS
LYMPH NODES

Stage 1: The cancer is small (no larger than 3 cm for stage 1A; up to 5 cm for stage 1B) and has not spread to the lymph nodes.

Stage 2: The tumor is up to 7 cm in diameter and may have spread to nearby lymph nodes.

Stage 3A: The cancer has started to extend into surrounding tissues and structures, such as the lining of the lung and chest wall, and has spread to lymph nodes on the same side of the chest as the tumor.

TREATMENT OPTIONS:

SURGERY

ADJUVANT CHEMOTHERAPY

RADIATION THERAPY & CHEMOTHERAPY

CANCER STAGING

2

BRAIN

Stage 4:
The cancer has spread to form new tumors in other parts of the body, such as the bone, brain, liver, and adrenal gland.

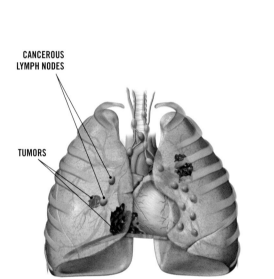

CANCEROUS
LYMPH NODES

TUMORS

BONE

LIVER

ADRENAL
GLAND

Stage 3B: Two or more tumors are present, and the cancer has spread to the lung and lymph nodes on the opposite side of the chest.

ILLUSTRATION BY ERIN MOORE

Colon Cancer

There are several systems to stage colon cancer, but the most commonly used system was developed by the American Joint Committee on Cancer.

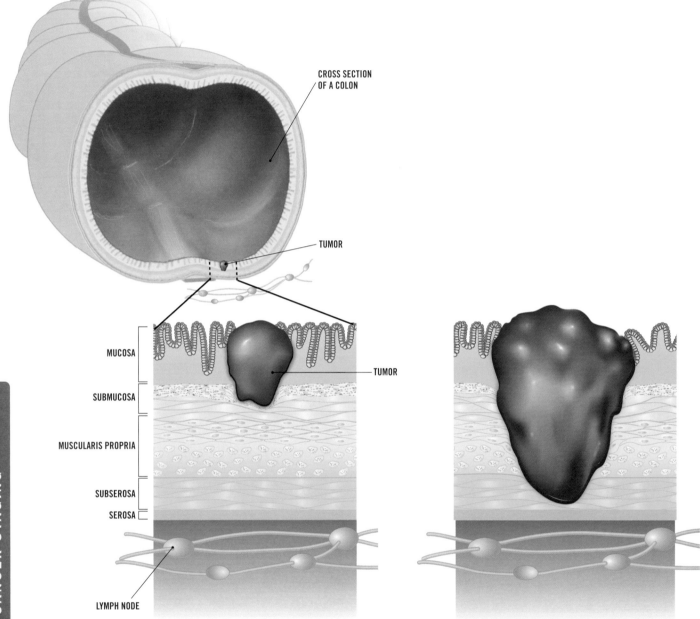

CROSS SECTION OF A COLON

TUMOR

MUCOSA

SUBMUCOSA

MUSCULARIS PROPRIA

SUBSEROSA

SEROSA

TUMOR

LYMPH NODE

STAGE 1: The cancer has grown through the mucosa, or inner layer of the colon, and extends to the submucosa.

STAGE 2: The cancer has grown through the submucosa and into the next layer, the muscularis propria. It may or may not extend into the next layers, the subserosa or serosa, or to nearby tissues or organs. It has not spread to the lymph nodes.

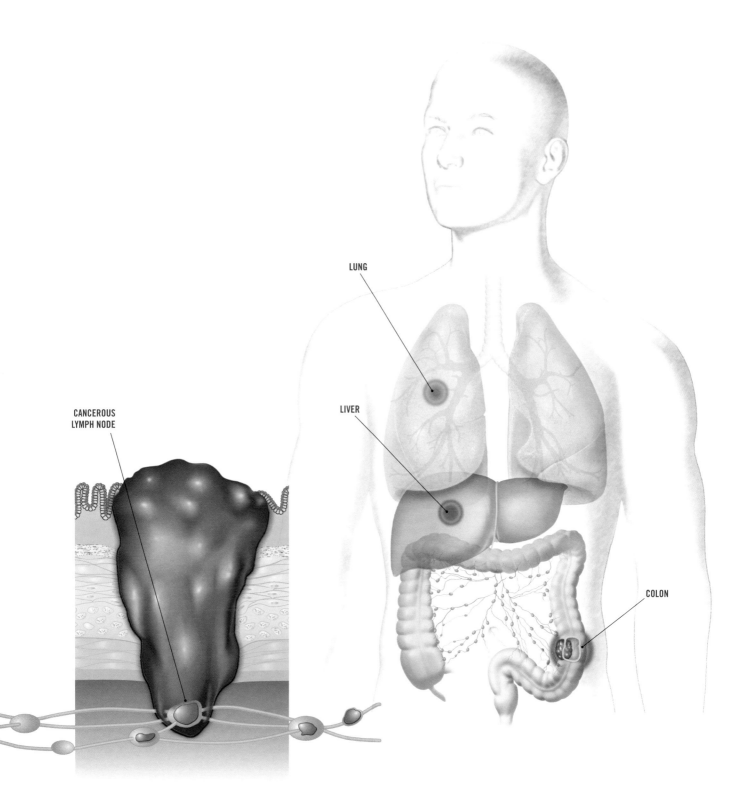

CANCEROUS LYMPH NODE

LUNG

LIVER

COLON

STAGE 3: The cancer may or may not have grown through the wall of the colon, but it has spread to nearby lymph nodes. It has not spread to distant tissues or organs.

STAGE 4: The cancer has spread to distant sites, such as the liver or lung. It may or may not have grown through the wall of the colon. It may or may not have spread to nearby lymph nodes.

Chronic Lymphocytic Leukemia

The Rai staging system is typically used to describe chronic lymphocytic leukemia, a cancer of the blood.

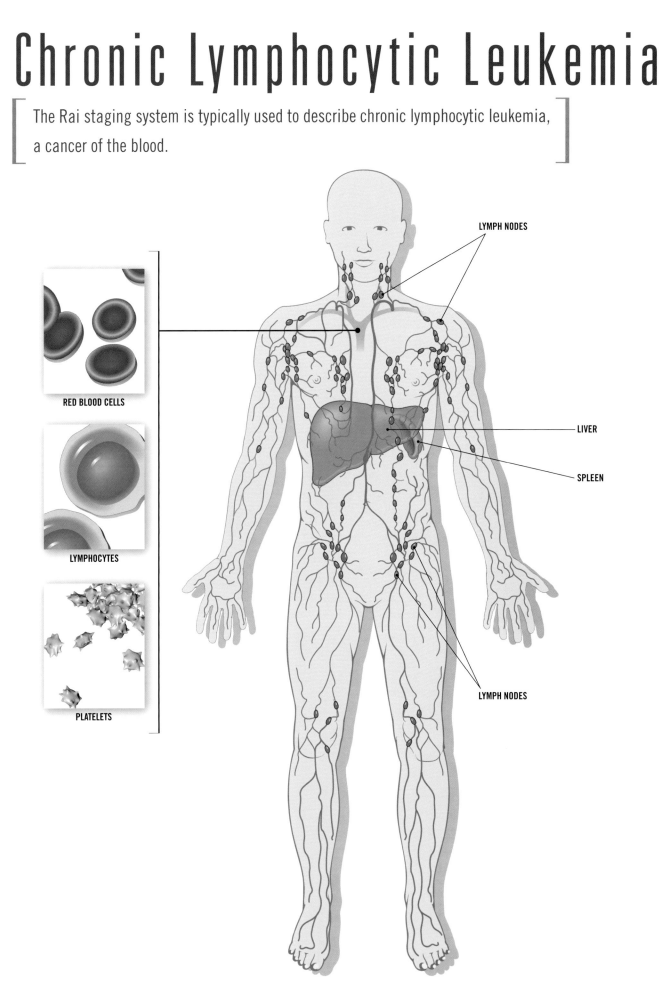

RED BLOOD CELLS

LYMPHOCYTES

PLATELETS

LYMPH NODES

LYMPH NODES

LIVER

SPLEEN

2

The Rai staging system is used to describe chronic lymphocytic leukemia. Under this system, there are five stages:

STAGE 0:

A high number of lymphocytes, a type of white blood cell, are found in the blood, a condition called lymphocytosis (a lymphocyte count greater than 15,000 cells per cubic millimeter). In this stage, the lymph nodes, spleen, and liver are not enlarged. Red blood cell and platelet counts are in normal range.

STAGE 1:

In addition to lymphocytosis, the lymph nodes are swollen. The spleen and liver are not enlarged. Red blood cell and platelet counts are in normal range.

STAGE 2:

In addition to lymphocytosis, the spleen and/or liver are enlarged. The lymph nodes may or may not be swollen. Red blood cell and platelet counts are in normal range.

STAGE 3:

In addition to lymphocytosis, red blood cell counts are low, a condition called anemia. The spleen and/or liver may or may not be enlarged. The lymph nodes may or may not be swollen. Platelet counts are in normal range.

STAGE 4:

In addition to lymphocytosis, platelet counts are low, a condition called thrombocytopenia. The spleen and/or liver may or may not be enlarged. The lymph nodes may or may not be swollen. Red blood cell counts may or may not be low.

In addition, health care providers may divide these stages into risk groups when discussing treatment options. Stage 0 is regarded as low risk. Stage 1 and 2 are regarded as intermediate risk. Stage 3 and 4 are regarded as high risk.

Non-Hodgkin Lymphoma

The Ann Arbor staging system is used to describe the stages of non-Hodgkin lymphoma in adults.

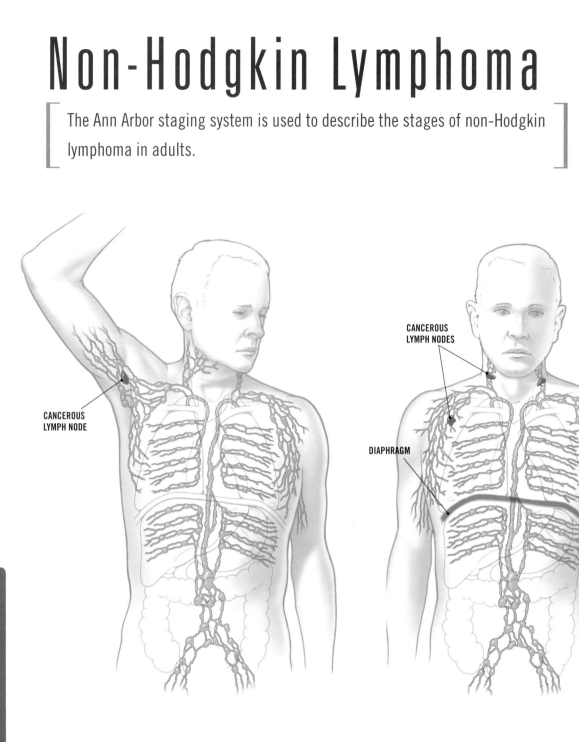

CANCEROUS LYMPH NODE

CANCEROUS LYMPH NODES

DIAPHRAGM

STAGE 1:
The cancer is located in a lymph node or nodes in a single lymph node group.

STAGE 1E:
The cancer is located in one organ or in one area outside the lymph nodes (extranodal).

STAGE 2:
The cancer is located in two or more lymph node groups on the same side of the diaphragm.

STAGE 2E:
The cancer is located in one or more lymph node groups on the same side of the diaphragm and in an organ or area outside the lymph nodes.

2

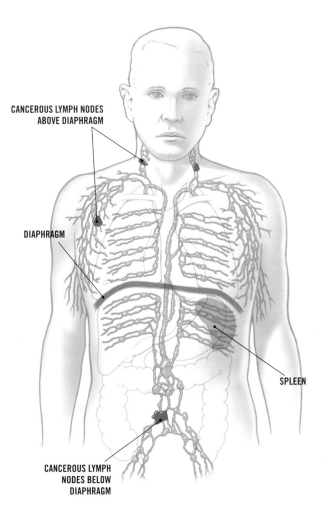

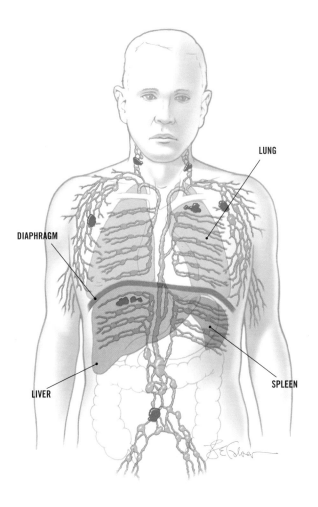

STAGE 3: The cancer is located in one or more lymph node groups above and below the diaphragm.

STAGE 3E: The cancer is located in lymph node groups above and below the diaphragm and in an organ or area outside the lymph nodes.

STAGE 3S: The cancer is located in lymph node groups above and below the diaphragm and in the spleen.

STAGE 3S+E: The cancer is located in lymph node groups above and below the diaphragm, in the spleen, and in an organ or area outside the lymph nodes.

STAGE 4:

The cancer has spread outside the lymph nodes to one or more distant organs, such as the liver, lung, or bone marrow.

Melanoma

To define the development of melanoma and determine the treatment course, experts have outlined the following staging system.

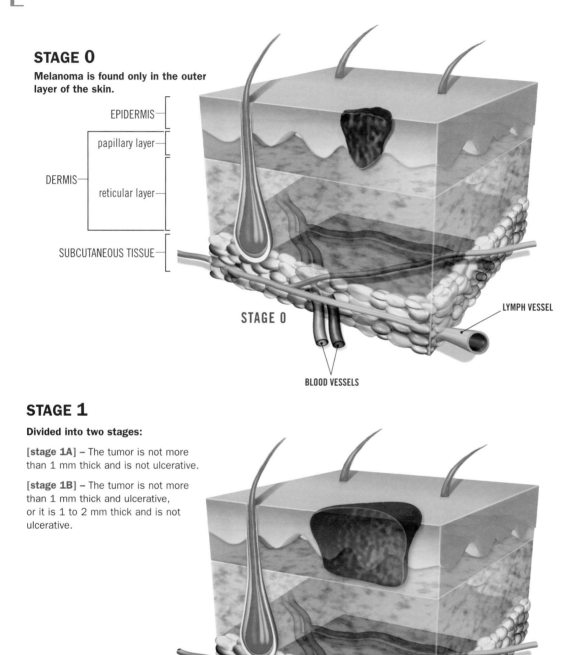

STAGE 0

Melanoma is found only in the outer layer of the skin.

EPIDERMIS

papillary layer

DERMIS

reticular layer

SUBCUTANEOUS TISSUE

STAGE 0

LYMPH VESSEL

BLOOD VESSELS

STAGE 1

Divided into two stages:

[stage 1A] – The tumor is not more than 1 mm thick and is not ulcerative.

[stage 1B] – The tumor is not more than 1 mm thick and ulcerative, or it is 1 to 2 mm thick and is not ulcerative.

STAGE 1A

CANCER STAGING

2

STAGE 2

Divided into three stages:

[stage 2A] – The tumor is 1 to 2 mm thick with ulceration, or 2 to 4 mm thick with no ulceration.

[stage 2B] – The tumor is 2 to 4 mm thick with ulceration, or more than 4 mm thick with no ulceration.

[stage 2C] – The tumor is more than 4 mm thick and ulcerative.

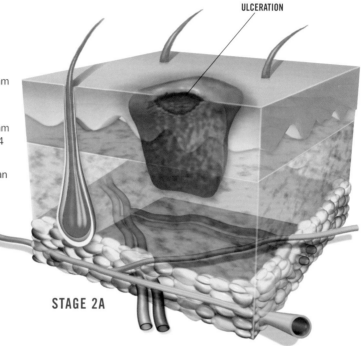

ULCERATION

STAGE 2A

STAGE 3

The tumor may be of any thickness, with or without ulceration, and has spread to one or more nearby lymph nodes; divided into three stages:

[stage 3A] – The tumor may have spread to as many as three lymph nodes, but the tumor in the lymph node can only be seen under a microscope.

[stage 3B] – The tumor has spread to as many as three lymph nodes, or the melanoma has not spread to the lymph nodes but has produced satellite tumors.

[stage 3C] – The tumor has spread to four or more lymph nodes or has clinically evident positive lymph nodes.

Melanoma spreads through lymph vessel to regional **lymph node**

STAGE 3

STAGE 4

The melanoma has spread to other organs and lymph nodes away from the original site.

Chapter 3

Causes&Risks

CANCER CELLS emerge because of changes or alterations to DNA, the genetic blueprint that instructs cell growth. Usually the body is able to repair altered DNA, but in cancer cells, the damaged DNA cannot be repaired. In some cases, people inherit altered DNA, which may develop into cancer. More commonly, a person's DNA is changed by exposure to environmental factors or by random cellular events. For example, although most cases of lung cancer can be attributed to smoking, other risk factors may include having a lung disease such as chronic obstructive pulmonary disease, genetic susceptibility to lung cancer, or exposure to secondhand smoke, radon gas, asbestos, or other chemicals.

Lung Cancer in Nonsmokers

[Lung cancer in never-smokers can be caused by a number of environmental triggers, such as secondhand smoke, cooking fumes, asbestos, and various cancer-causing chemicals.]

❷ Human papillomavirus: Research has found an association, mainly among Asians, between HPV and lung tumors in never-smokers. HPV types 16 and 18, which are also linked to cervical, vulvar, and head and neck cancers, appear to be the most common offenders.

❶ Estrogen: Because two-thirds of never-smokers diagnosed with lung cancer are women, estrogen is thought to play a role in the same way it's proven to promote proliferation of breast cancer cells.

❸ Mutations of EGFR: Activation of the epidermal growth factor receptor triggers DNA replication and cell division, and tumors with mutations in the gene for EGFR are found most often in women, Asians, and never-smokers. These patients respond particularly well to EGFR inhibitors.

FURTHER distinguished by its histologic type, lung cancer in never-smokers is most often a type of non-small cell lung cancer called adenocarcinoma, while smoker diagnoses are more evenly divided among adenocarcinoma and squamous cell carcinoma, another type of non-small cell lung cancer.

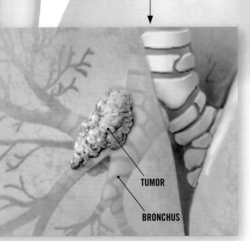

TUMOR

BRONCHUS

Squamous cell carcinomas are found centrally in the lung near the bronchi.
NEVER-SMOKERS: 6% [SMOKERS: 36%]

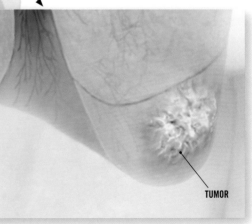

TUMOR

Adenocarcinomas are found near the edge of the lung.
NEVER-SMOKERS: 70% [SMOKERS: 40%]

ILLUSTRATION BY PAM CURRY

Evolution of Liver Cancer

[Liver cancer, also known as hepatocellular carcinoma, can be caused by hepatitis B and C or chronic alcohol use.]

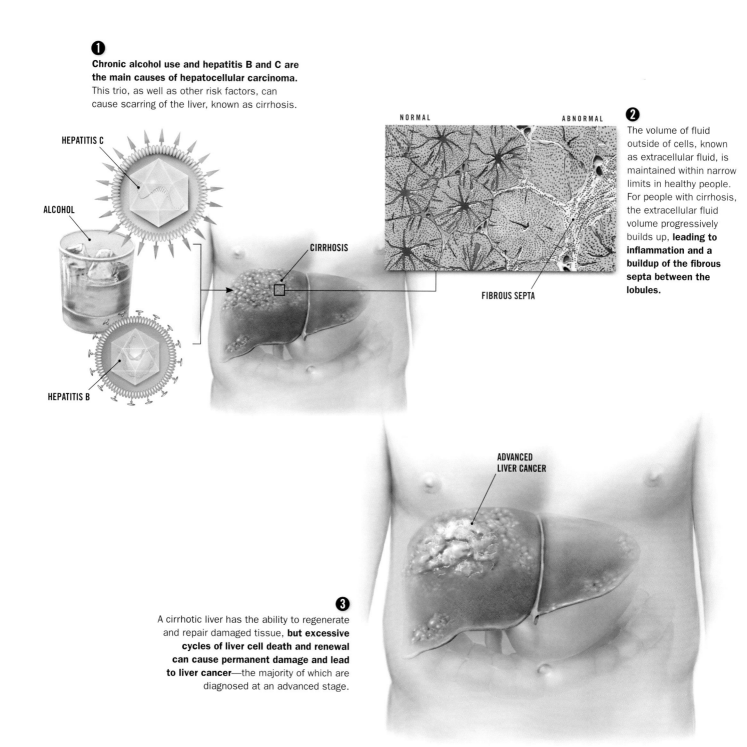

❶ Chronic alcohol use and hepatitis B and C are the main causes of hepatocellular carcinoma. This trio, as well as other risk factors, can cause scarring of the liver, known as cirrhosis.

HEPATITIS C

ALCOHOL

HEPATITIS B

CIRRHOSIS

NORMAL   ABNORMAL

FIBROUS SEPTA

❷ The volume of fluid outside of cells, known as extracellular fluid, is maintained within narrow limits in healthy people. For people with cirrhosis, the extracellular fluid volume progressively builds up, **leading to inflammation and a buildup of the fibrous septa between the lobules.**

ADVANCED LIVER CANCER

❸ A cirrhotic liver has the ability to regenerate and repair damaged tissue, **but excessive cycles of liver cell death and renewal can cause permanent damage and lead to liver cancer**—the majority of which are diagnosed at an advanced stage.

Inflammation

Chronic inflammation can trigger the immune system to battle against a persistent viral infection or bacterium and can contribute to the development of cancer.

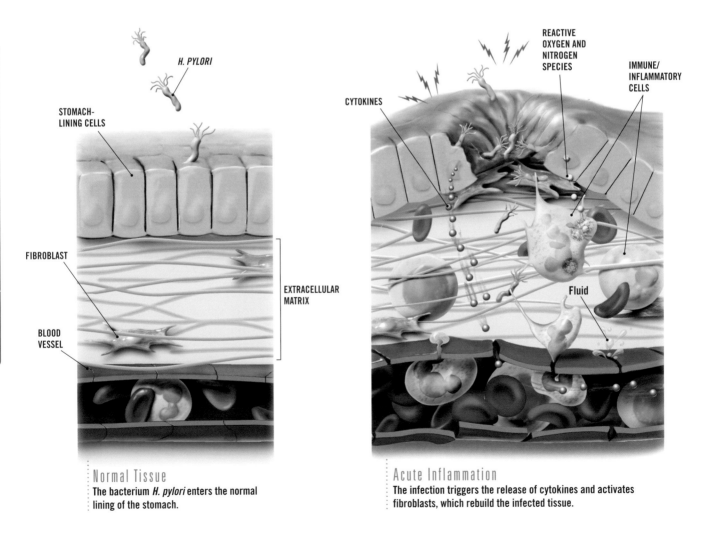

Normal Tissue
The bacterium *H. pylori* enters the normal lining of the stomach.

Acute Inflammation
The infection triggers the release of cytokines and activates fibroblasts, which rebuild the infected tissue.

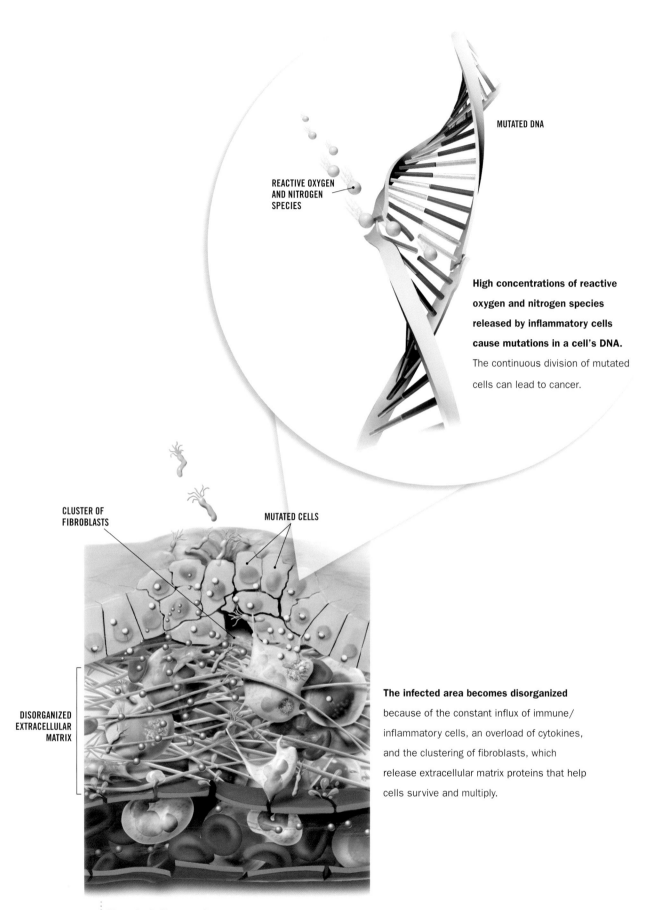

MUTATED DNA

REACTIVE OXYGEN AND NITROGEN SPECIES

High concentrations of reactive oxygen and nitrogen species released by inflammatory cells cause mutations in a cell's DNA. The continuous division of mutated cells can lead to cancer.

CLUSTER OF FIBROBLASTS

MUTATED CELLS

DISORGANIZED EXTRACELLULAR MATRIX

The infected area becomes disorganized because of the constant influx of immune/ inflammatory cells, an overload of cytokines, and the clustering of fibroblasts, which release extracellular matrix proteins that help cells survive and multiply.

Chronic Inflammation

Inflammation goes from acute to chronic if it doesn't resolve or becomes uncontrollable because of repeated tissue damage from the *H. pylori* infection or because of other disorders in the inflammatory process.

Estrogen's Effects

The effects of natural estrogen are seen throughout the body. Hormone replacement therapy may be used to sustain these effects but may also increase the risk of breast cancer growth.

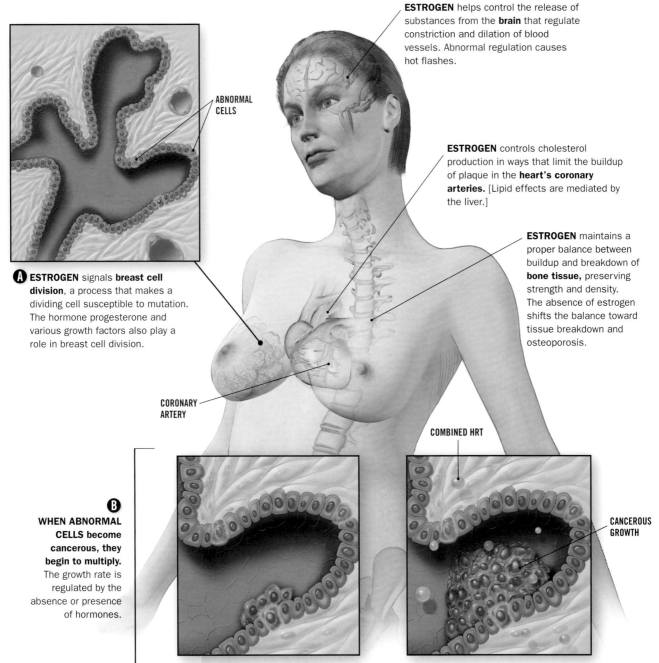

ESTROGEN helps control the release of substances from the **brain** that regulate constriction and dilation of blood vessels. Abnormal regulation causes hot flashes.

ESTROGEN controls cholesterol production in ways that limit the buildup of plaque in the **heart's coronary arteries.** [Lipid effects are mediated by the liver.]

ESTROGEN maintains a proper balance between buildup and breakdown of **bone tissue,** preserving strength and density. The absence of estrogen shifts the balance toward tissue breakdown and osteoporosis.

ABNORMAL CELLS

A **ESTROGEN** signals **breast cell division**, a process that makes a dividing cell susceptible to mutation. The hormone progesterone and various growth factors also play a role in breast cell division.

CORONARY ARTERY

COMBINED HRT

CANCEROUS GROWTH

B **WHEN ABNORMAL CELLS become cancerous, they begin to multiply.** The growth rate is regulated by the absence or presence of hormones.

In the absence of hormone replacement therapy (HRT), the mutated cell multiplies at a normal rate.

When combined HRT [estrogen and progestin] is introduced into a woman's body, the mutated breast cell grows rapidly, fueled by the hormones.

CAUSES & RISKS

3

CURE's
Illustrated
Guide
to Cancer

Chapter 4

Symptoms &
Diagnosis

SYMPTOMS of cancer can range from palpable, such as a lump, to vague, such as fatigue.

Some symptoms are specific to certain cancers. For example, blood in the urine or pain during

urination may be a sign of bladder cancer, but they could also be symptoms of other diseases,

such as a urinary tract infection. Diagnostic tests help physicians find cancer and determine

treatment. X-rays, CT scans, and PET scans may be used to detect cancer. A pathologist may

examine blood samples or tissue from biopsies to diagnose cancer. There are other diag-

nostic tests available, and many new tests are being developed to help physicians identify,

analyze, and treat cancer.

Cancers of Unknown Origin

For patients diagnosed with metastatic cancer, the origin of the cancer may be difficult to locate. A variety of diagnostic tests can help doctors pinpoint where the cancer started.

The first level of testing looks at the **big picture**

The second level takes an **inside look** at the cancer cells

The third level involves tests that determine the **genetic makeup** of the cancer

Chest X-ray:
Helps determine if cancer is present in the lung.

CT scan:
Provides a detailed cross-section image of parts of the body to locate tumors.

PET scan:
Detects tumors and determines how far the cancer has spread by measuring sugar absorption in the body's tissues.

Histology:
Based on how the cells look under the microscope, cancers are assigned to a subset with a specific treatment plan.

Fluorescent in situ hybridization:
Uses fluorescent molecules to detect the number of cancer-related genes and their chromosomal positions in tumor cells.

Immuno-histochemistry:
A staining test that can identify cancer cells by the characteristic proteins on the cell surface and within the nucleus or cytoplasm.

Gene expression profiling:
Determines patterns of gene activity in the metastatic cancer and makes the best match based on typical patterns known for primary cancer of specific sites.

IMAGE COURTESY OF PATHWORK DIAGNOSTICS

Despite extensive testing, the origin of the cancer remains unknown in about **4 percent** of patients.

Diagnosing Sarcoma

[Sarcoma develops in connective tissues, such as the bone or muscle, and can be diagnosed with a variety of tests.]

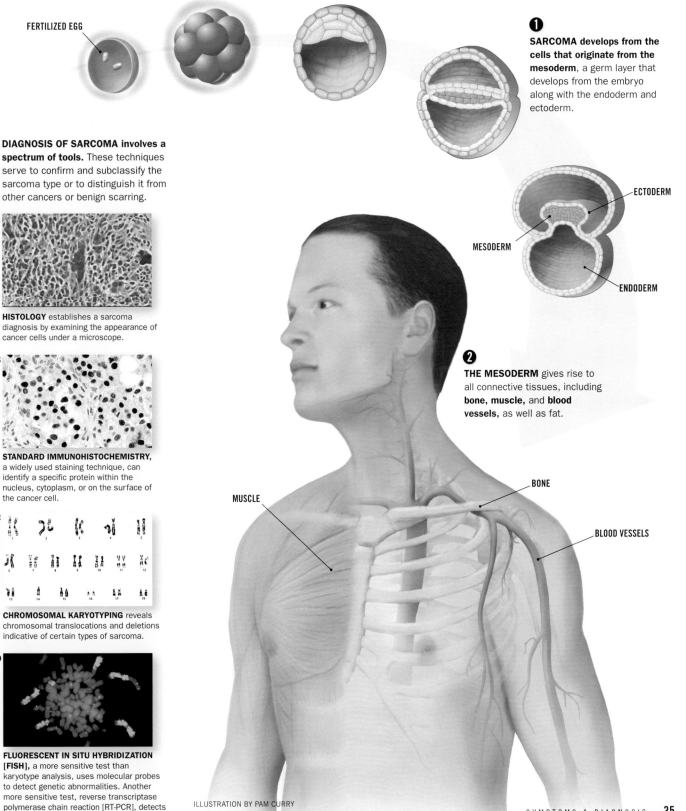

FERTILIZED EGG

❶

SARCOMA develops from the cells that originate from the mesoderm, a germ layer that develops from the embryo along with the endoderm and ectoderm.

ECTODERM

MESODERM

ENDODERM

DIAGNOSIS OF SARCOMA involves a spectrum of tools. These techniques serve to confirm and subclassify the sarcoma type or to distinguish it from other cancers or benign scarring.

A

HISTOLOGY establishes a sarcoma diagnosis by examining the appearance of cancer cells under a microscope.

B

STANDARD IMMUNOHISTOCHEMISTRY, a widely used staining technique, can identify a specific protein within the nucleus, cytoplasm, or on the surface of the cancer cell.

C

CHROMOSOMAL KARYOTYPING reveals chromosomal translocations and deletions indicative of certain types of sarcoma.

D

FLUORESCENT IN SITU HYBRIDIZATION [FISH], a more sensitive test than karyotype analysis, uses molecular probes to detect genetic abnormalities. Another more sensitive test, reverse transcriptase polymerase chain reaction [RT-PCR], detects small deletions and point mutations.

❷

THE MESODERM gives rise to all connective tissues, including **bone, muscle,** and **blood vessels,** as well as fat.

BONE

MUSCLE

BLOOD VESSELS

Image A courtesy of Naseem Uddin, MD; Image B reprinted with permission from C.R. Antonescu, "The role of genetic testing in soft tissue sarcoma," *Histopathology*, 2006; Images C and D courtesy of Jonathan A. Fletcher, MD

ILLUSTRATION BY PAM CURRY

Ovarian Cancer Symptoms

As a tumor in the ovary spreads, it can cause a variety of symptoms that are specifically related to the tumor.

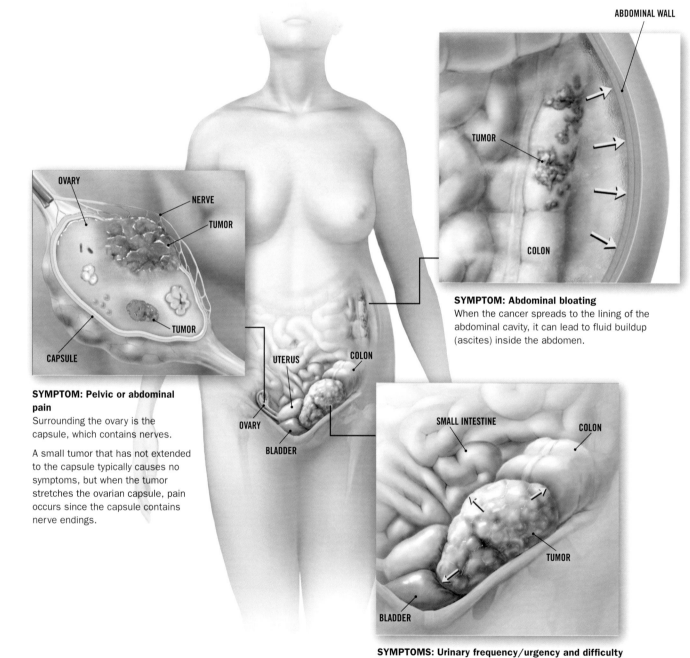

ABDOMINAL WALL

TUMOR

COLON

OVARY

NERVE

TUMOR

TUMOR

CAPSULE

UTERUS

COLON

OVARY

BLADDER

SMALL INTESTINE

COLON

TUMOR

BLADDER

SYMPTOM: Pelvic or abdominal pain

Surrounding the ovary is the capsule, which contains nerves.

A small tumor that has not extended to the capsule typically causes no symptoms, but when the tumor stretches the ovarian capsule, pain occurs since the capsule contains nerve endings.

SYMPTOM: Abdominal bloating

When the cancer spreads to the lining of the abdominal cavity, it can lead to fluid buildup (ascites) inside the abdomen.

SYMPTOMS: Urinary frequency/urgency and difficulty eating

An advanced tumor can block the intestinal tract, causing the patient to feel full too quickly after eating and to experience bloating and other abdominal symptoms.

Urinary frequency or urgency occurs when the tumor puts excessive pressure on the bladder.

ILLUSTRATION BY PAM CURRY

Oncotype DX

Oncotype DX is a test that allows hormone-positive breast cancer patients to obtain a refined risk assessment that predicts their risk of recurrence and whether chemotherapy will reduce that risk.

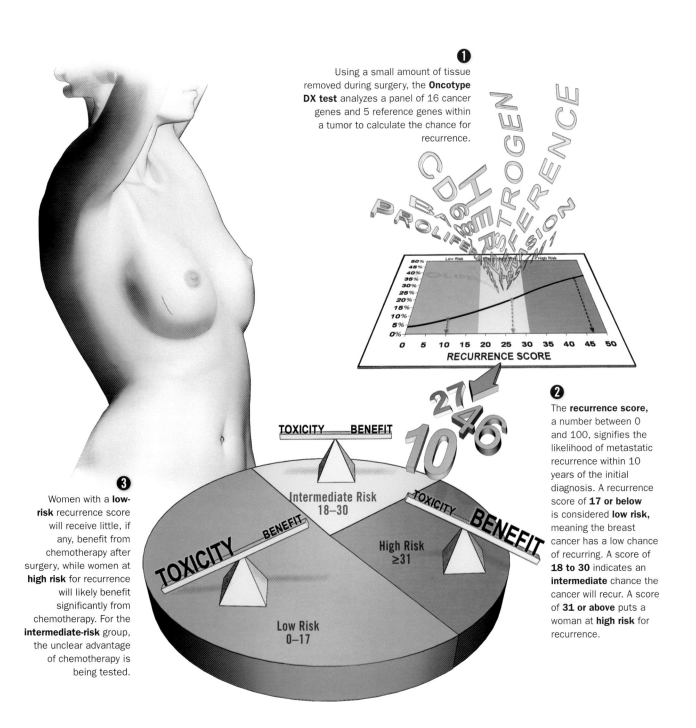

❶ Using a small amount of tissue removed during surgery, the **Oncotype DX test** analyzes a panel of 16 cancer genes and 5 reference genes within a tumor to calculate the chance for recurrence.

❷ The **recurrence score,** a number between 0 and 100, signifies the likelihood of metastatic recurrence within 10 years of the initial diagnosis. A recurrence score of **17 or below** is considered **low risk,** meaning the breast cancer has a low chance of recurring. A score of **18 to 30** indicates an **intermediate** chance the cancer will recur. A score of **31 or above** puts a woman at **high risk** for recurrence.

❸ Women with a **low-risk** recurrence score will receive little, if any, benefit from chemotherapy after surgery, while women at **high risk** for recurrence will likely benefit significantly from chemotherapy. For the **intermediate-risk** group, the unclear advantage of chemotherapy is being tested.

RECURRENCE SCORE

TOXICITY BENEFIT

Intermediate Risk 18–30

High Risk ≥31

Low Risk 0–17

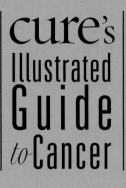

Chapter 5

Treatments

TREATMENT for cancer may include surgery, radiation therapy, chemotherapy, hormonal therapy, stem cell transplantation, biological therapies, or a combination of these treatments. In some cases, patients may have several treatment options. It is important that patients understand the possible benefits of each treatment, as well as the side effects and risks. If a patient has few options or wants to try an experimental treatment, he or she can consider enrolling in a clinical trial. Clinical trials test new, experimental treatments to determine whether they are more effective than what is currently available, if they have fewer side effects, or whether they are more convenient, such as medications taken by mouth or those with shorter treatment times. Search for clinical trials at www.curetoday.com/trialcheck.

Mohs Surgery

[The Mohs technique is used to remove certain types of cancer, layer by layer, such as skin cancer.]

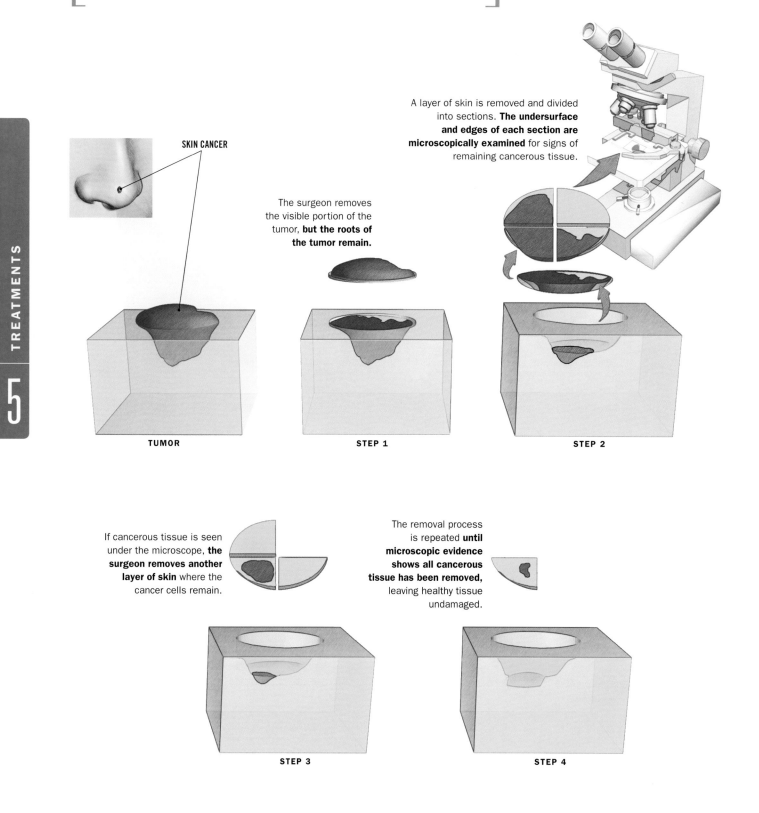

SKIN CANCER

A layer of skin is removed and divided into sections. **The undersurface and edges of each section are microscopically examined** for signs of remaining cancerous tissue.

The surgeon removes the visible portion of the tumor, **but the roots of the tumor remain.**

TUMOR

STEP 1

STEP 2

If cancerous tissue is seen under the microscope, **the surgeon removes another layer of skin** where the cancer cells remain.

The removal process is repeated **until microscopic evidence shows all cancerous tissue has been removed,** leaving healthy tissue undamaged.

STEP 3

STEP 4

ILLUSTRATION BY ERIN MOORE

TREATMENTS

5

da Vinci Surgical System

The da Vinci robot is a minimally invasive surgical technique that is used for a variety of procedures, including prostatectomy for prostate cancer.

 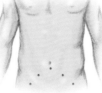

TYPICAL INCISION   DA VINCI INCISIONS

IN TRADITIONAL prostate surgery, surgeons make an 8- to 10-inch incision on the lower abdomen versus **da Vinci's five 1- to 2-cm incisions,** which result in less blood loss.

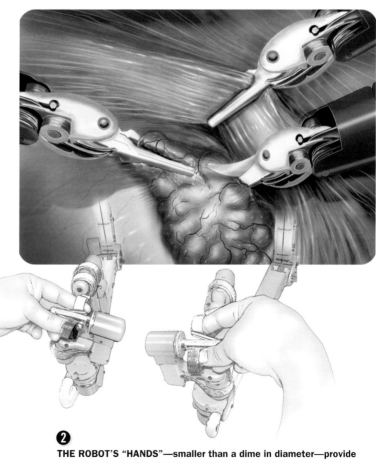

❶
THE SURGEON leads the procedure from a console a few feet away from the patient. **The hand controls provide precise direction of the surgeon's movements,** filtering out hand tremors and translating large hand movements to micro-movements.

❷
THE ROBOT'S "HANDS"—smaller than a dime in diameter—provide a greater range of motion than the human hand to remove cancerous tissue from the prostate. After the tumor is separated from surrounding tissues, it's placed in a plastic pouch attached to a string, then pulled out through the middle incision near the navel.

ILLUSTRATION BY ERIN MOORE

Kidney Surgery

A partial nephrectomy is a surgical technique used to remove tumors from the kidney while preserving healthy tissue, as opposed to removing the entire kidney.

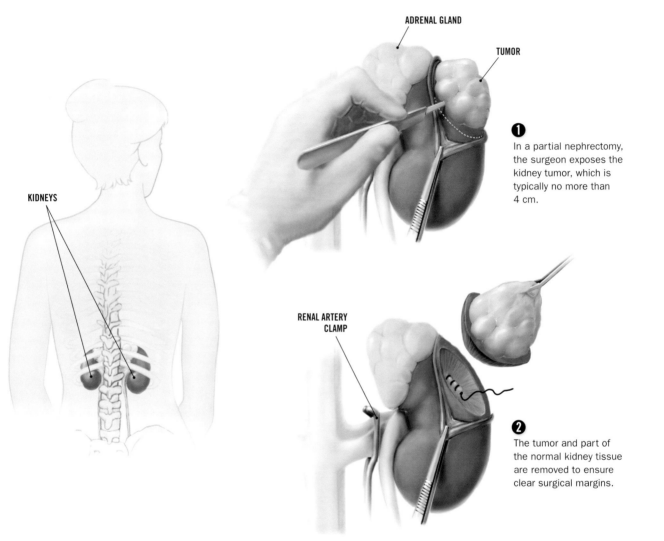

KIDNEYS

ADRENAL GLAND

TUMOR

❶ In a partial nephrectomy, the surgeon exposes the kidney tumor, which is typically no more than 4 cm.

RENAL ARTERY CLAMP

❷ The tumor and part of the normal kidney tissue are removed to ensure clear surgical margins.

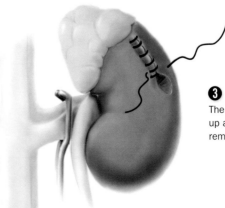

❸ The kidney is sewn up and renal function remains unaffected.

ILLUSTRATION BY PAM CURRY

Stem Cell Transplant

The doses of chemotherapy and radiation used to treat some cancers, particularly leukemias and lymphomas, can damage stem cells. Stem cell transplants introduce healthy cells back into the body.

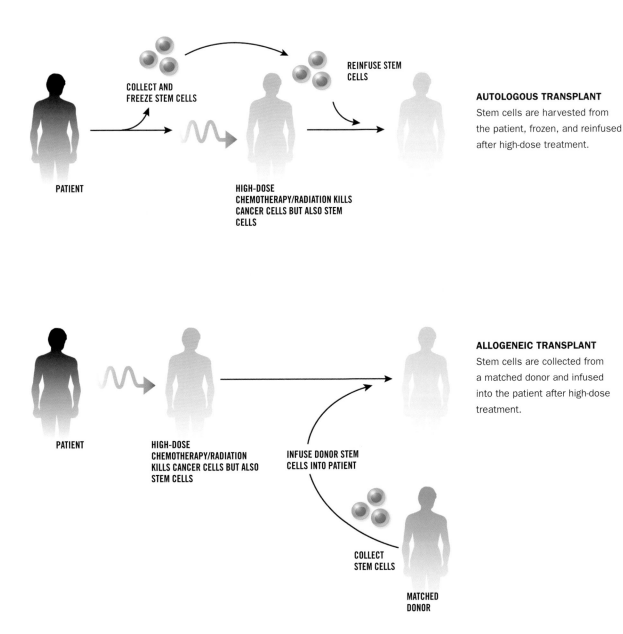

COLLECT AND FREEZE STEM CELLS

REINFUSE STEM CELLS

PATIENT

HIGH-DOSE CHEMOTHERAPY/RADIATION KILLS CANCER CELLS BUT ALSO STEM CELLS

AUTOLOGOUS TRANSPLANT
Stem cells are harvested from the patient, frozen, and reinfused after high-dose treatment.

PATIENT

HIGH-DOSE CHEMOTHERAPY/RADIATION KILLS CANCER CELLS BUT ALSO STEM CELLS

INFUSE DONOR STEM CELLS INTO PATIENT

COLLECT STEM CELLS

MATCHED DONOR

ALLOGENEIC TRANSPLANT
Stem cells are collected from a matched donor and infused into the patient after high-dose treatment.

Radiation Techniques

Traditional radiation therapy is useful in killing cancer cells but can also damage healthy tissue. New techniques are more precise, resulting in fewer side effects.

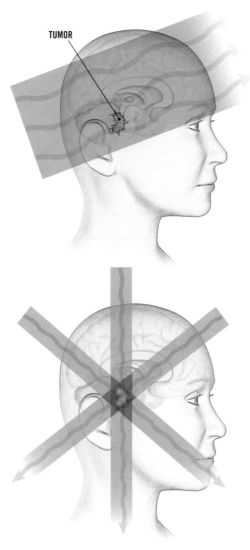

TUMOR

X-RAY BEAM

X-rays are high-energy photons (gamma rays) created by machines, and although the beam can be aimed at a tumor, the radiation dose is delivered to healthy tissue in front of and behind the tumor. The energy breaks DNA bonds, causing cell death.

STEREOTACTIC RADIOSURGERY

Stereotactic radiosurgery uses highly focused gamma rays that originate at different angles and intersect at the tumor site. The tumor is hit with a high, concentrated dose of radiation, sparing the surrounding healthy tissue from the full dose.

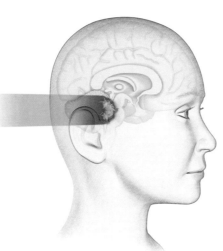

PROTON BEAM

The larger size of a proton particle ensures that the bulk of energy is deposited exactly at the tumor site, allowing more precise treatment and, in some cases, treatment of areas previously radiated with standard radiation therapy.

ILLUSTRATION BY ERIN MOORE

Brachytherapy

Brachytherapy delivers radiation directly to the tumor site. Mammosite, depicted below, is specific for breast cancer and uses radioactive seeds.

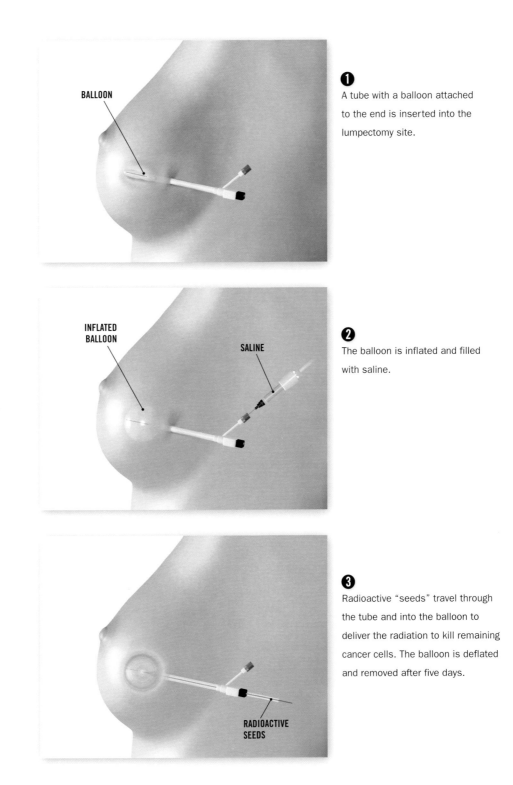

BALLOON

❶ A tube with a balloon attached to the end is inserted into the lumpectomy site.

INFLATED BALLOON

SALINE

❷ The balloon is inflated and filled with saline.

RADIOACTIVE SEEDS

❸ Radioactive "seeds" travel through the tube and into the balloon to deliver the radiation to kill remaining cancer cells. The balloon is deflated and removed after five days.

Targeted Therapies

[Cancer cells develop certain characteristics that allow them to grow and survive. These traits serve as the targets for a variety of cancer drugs.]

HORMONES
What Targeted Drugs Do: Block the effects of hormones that fuel the growth of some cancers

GROWTH FACTORS
What Targeted Drugs Do: Inhibit the signaling of growth factors that aid in the tumor's growth

ANGIOGENESIS
What Targeted Drugs Do: Block proteins that stimulate the growth of tumor-feeding blood vessels

PROLIFERATION
What Targeted Drugs Do: Hinder the ability of cancer cells to divide

METASTASIS
What Targeted Drugs Do: Prevent the migration of cancer cells from the primary tumor to distant sites

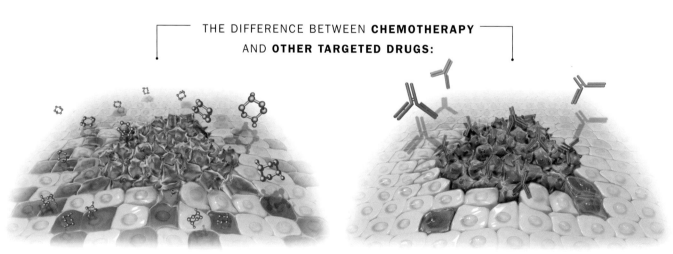

THE DIFFERENCE BETWEEN **CHEMOTHERAPY** AND **OTHER TARGETED DRUGS:**

CHEMOTHERAPY targets and kills not only rapidly dividing cancer cells but also dividing healthy cells, such as hair follicles.

TARGETED AGENTS, such as monoclonal antibodies, specifically target and kill cancer cells while sparing most healthy cells.

ILLUSTRATION BY ERIN MOORE

Thyroid Cancer Treatment

The thyroid gland naturally absorbs nearly all the iodine in the blood. Radioactive iodine therapy takes advantage of this to kill cancerous cells without affecting the rest of the body.

The Feedback Loop:

The hypothalamus produces thyrotropin-releasing hormone (TRH), which stimulates the pituitary gland to make thyroid-stimulating hormone (TSH).
1

HYPOTHALAMUS

PITUITARY GLAND

TRH

4
The hypothalamus senses the level of thyroid hormones in the body and mediates a feedback loop.

Low levels of thyroid hormones stimulate the production of TRH and subsequently higher levels of TSH and thyroid hormones.

High levels of thyroid hormones inhibit the production of TRH, thereby regulating thyroid function.

3

TSH causes the thyroid gland to produce thyroid hormones needed to regulate the body's metabolism.

THYROID HORMONES   TSH

THYROID GLAND

THYROID HORMONES

How Radioactive Iodine Therapy Works:

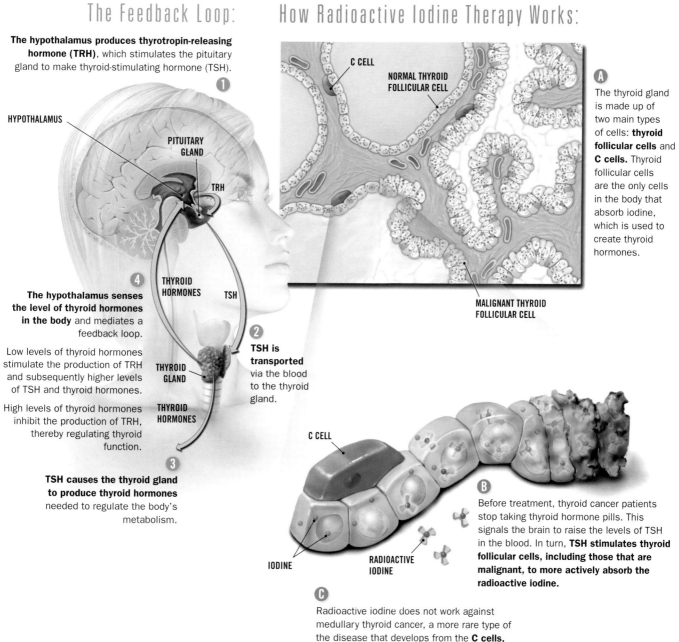

C CELL

NORMAL THYROID FOLLICULAR CELL

A
The thyroid gland is made up of two main types of cells: **thyroid follicular cells** and **C cells.** Thyroid follicular cells are the only cells in the body that absorb iodine, which is used to create thyroid hormones.

MALIGNANT THYROID FOLLICULAR CELL

2
TSH is transported via the blood to the thyroid gland.

C CELL

IODINE

RADIOACTIVE IODINE

B
Before treatment, thyroid cancer patients stop taking thyroid hormone pills. This signals the brain to raise the levels of TSH in the blood. In turn, **TSH stimulates thyroid follicular cells, including those that are malignant, to more actively absorb the radioactive iodine.**

C
Radioactive iodine does not work against medullary thyroid cancer, a more rare type of the disease that develops from the **C cells, which do not take up iodine.**

Brain Tumor Treatments

The tricky goal of gaining access to brain tumors has led to some unique approaches for treating cancer in the body's most complex organ.

❶ DIRECT EFFECT

The brain tumor has been surgically removed.

TREATMENT>

Biopolymer wafers are placed inside the resection area and deliver chemotherapy to the surrounding brain tissue. The risk of common complications, such as seizures and cerebral edema, has made this treatment option less desirable.

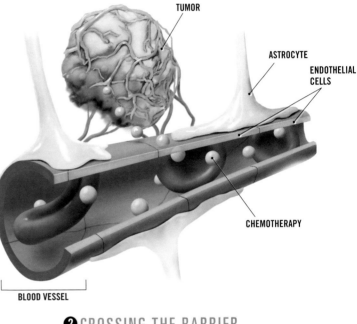

BIOPOLYMER WAFER

TUMOR

TUMOR

ASTROCYTE

ENDOTHELIAL CELLS

CHEMOTHERAPY

BLOOD VESSEL

❷ CROSSING THE BARRIER

The blood-brain barrier consists of tightly packed endothelial cells in brain capillaries and specialized brain cells called astrocytes.

TREATMENT>

Because of their molecular structure, some chemotherapies are able to pass through cell membranes to reach the tumor. Many other drugs are either too large or have a natural structure-related electrical charge that does not allow them to penetrate the membrane.

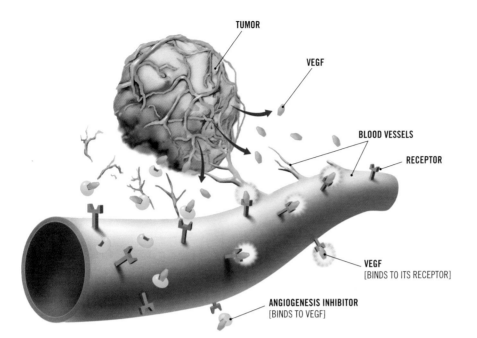

❸ STARVING THE TUMOR

The formation of new blood vessels to supply the tumor with oxygen and nutrients is caused by a process called angiogenesis.

TREATMENT>

Vascular endothelial growth factor [VEGF], a protein secreted by the tumor, binds to its receptor on endothelial cells that line blood vessel walls. Certain therapies, called angiogenesis inhibitors, can attach to VEGF and block this binding, thus stopping angiogenesis.

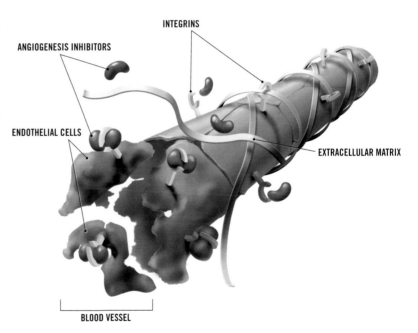

❹ CUTTING OFF THE BLOOD SUPPLY

Endothelial cells express integrins (protein receptors), which interact with the extracellular matrix and other endothelial cells to maintain the integrity of blood vessels.

TREATMENT>

One experimental angiogenesis inhibitor is designed to bind to integrins, which in turn release their hold on the extracellular matrix, causing the blood vessels feeding the tumor to fall apart.

Breast Cancer Treatments

Certain drugs target estrogen receptor-positive or HER2-positive breast cancers. Research is examining whether these two different therapies could be combined.

ESTROGEN RECEPTOR+

ESTROGEN

ESTROGEN RECEPTOR

DNA

1 In **estrogen-fueled breast cancer,** estrogen enters the cell and binds to the estrogen receptor before entering the nucleus and initiating cell division.

ANTI-ESTROGEN

2 Anti-estrogens bind to the estrogen receptor to prevent estrogen from initiating cell division.

THE OVARIES produce estrogen in premenopausal women, while **fat tissue** and the **adrenal glands** produce low levels of estrogen in postmenopausal women. Anti-estrogens block the effects of estrogen, while another class of agents, known as **aromatase inhibitors,** prevents creation of the hormone.

ANDROGEN

AROMATASE

AROMATASE INHIBITOR

ESTROGEN

1 **Aromatase** is the enzyme that converts androgen to estrogen in postmenopausal women.

2 **Aromatase inhibitors** block this conversion by binding to aromatase.

HER2 RECEPTOR+

EPIDERMAL GROWTH FACTOR

HER2 RECEPTOR

HER1/HER2 RECEPTOR

DNA

1 In **HER2-fueled breast cancer,** overabundant HER2 sends surplus growth signals that trigger rapid cell division.

TARGETED DRUG

TARGETED DRUG

2 **Different drugs** target the cancer through different pathways. One blocks the signaling by binding to the outside of the HER2 receptor, while another binds to the inner portion of both HER1 and HER2 to block signaling.

TUMOR

ADRENAL GLANDS

KIDNEY

FAT TISSUE

OVARY

SO HOW DO CANCER CELL RECEPTORS CROSS-TALK?

IN WOMEN WITH ESTROGEN RECEPTOR-POSITIVE BREAST CANCER, cross-talk can sometimes limit a drug's inhibition of the estrogen receptor growth pathway and can instead cause **the drug to initiate signaling communication with various growth factors, including HER2.** The net result is a new pathway for cancer growth.

ILLUSTRATION BY PAM CURRY

PARP Inhibitors

PARP inhibitors block an enzyme that repairs DNA damage and are particularly effective against breast cancer with BRCA1 and BRCA2 gene mutations.

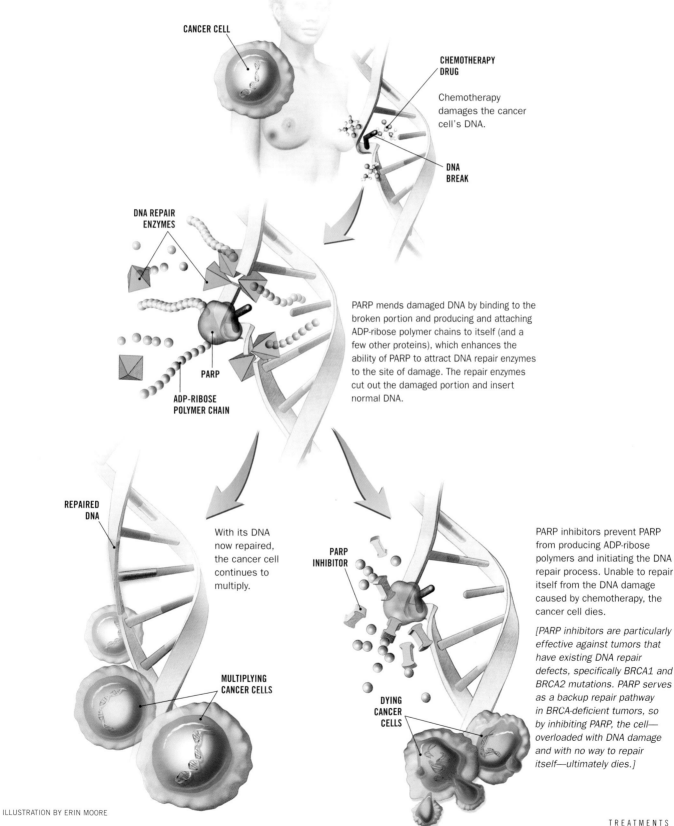

CANCER CELL

CHEMOTHERAPY DRUG

Chemotherapy damages the cancer cell's DNA.

DNA BREAK

DNA REPAIR ENZYMES

PARP mends damaged DNA by binding to the broken portion and producing and attaching ADP-ribose polymer chains to itself (and a few other proteins), which enhances the ability of PARP to attract DNA repair enzymes to the site of damage. The repair enzymes cut out the damaged portion and insert normal DNA.

PARP

ADP-RIBOSE POLYMER CHAIN

REPAIRED DNA

With its DNA now repaired, the cancer cell continues to multiply.

PARP INHIBITOR

PARP inhibitors prevent PARP from producing ADP-ribose polymers and initiating the DNA repair process. Unable to repair itself from the DNA damage caused by chemotherapy, the cancer cell dies.

[PARP inhibitors are particularly effective against tumors that have existing DNA repair defects, specifically BRCA1 and BRCA2 mutations. PARP serves as a backup repair pathway in BRCA-deficient tumors, so by inhibiting PARP, the cell—overloaded with DNA damage and with no way to repair itself—ultimately dies.]

MULTIPLYING CANCER CELLS

DYING CANCER CELLS

ILLUSTRATION BY ERIN MOORE

Non-Hodgkin Lymphoma Treatments

Cell division inhibitors get inside the cell to kill the cancer, while monoclonal antibodies target specific receptors on lymphoma cells to initiate an immune response against the cancer.

Non-Hodgkin lymphoma originates in the cells [lymphocytes] of the immune system and results in tumors in the **lymph nodes** and the **spleen.**

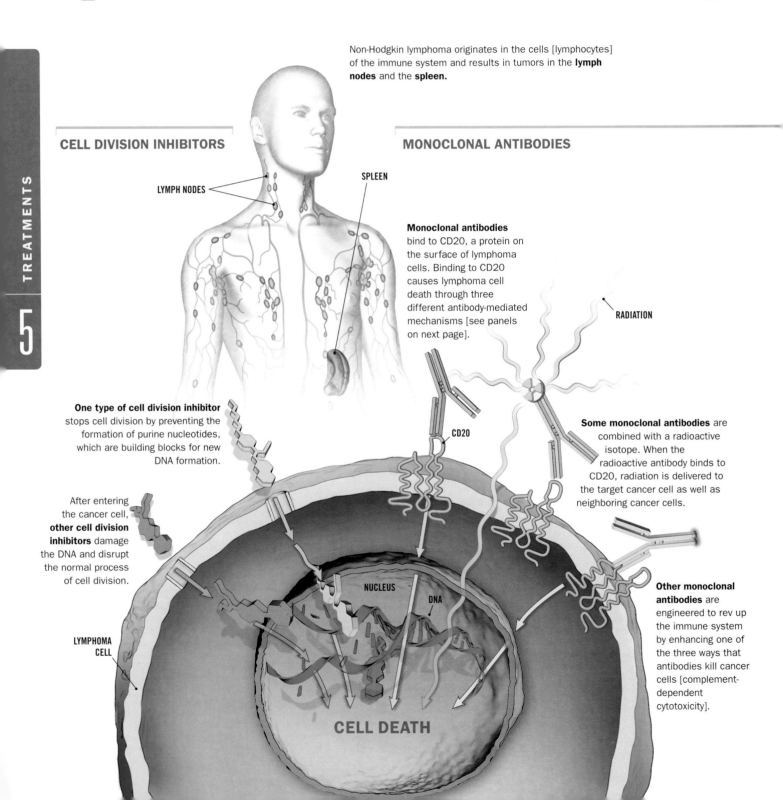

CELL DIVISION INHIBITORS

MONOCLONAL ANTIBODIES

LYMPH NODES

SPLEEN

Monoclonal antibodies bind to CD20, a protein on the surface of lymphoma cells. Binding to CD20 causes lymphoma cell death through three different antibody-mediated mechanisms [see panels on next page].

RADIATION

CD20

One type of cell division inhibitor stops cell division by preventing the formation of purine nucleotides, which are building blocks for new DNA formation.

Some monoclonal antibodies are combined with a radioactive isotope. When the radioactive antibody binds to CD20, radiation is delivered to the target cancer cell as well as neighboring cancer cells.

After entering the cancer cell, **other cell division inhibitors** damage the DNA and disrupt the normal process of cell division.

NUCLEUS

DNA

Other monoclonal antibodies are engineered to rev up the immune system by enhancing one of the three ways that antibodies kill cancer cells [complement-dependent cytotoxicity].

LYMPHOMA CELL

CELL DEATH

The **3** Ways Monoclonal Antibodies Kill Cancer Cells

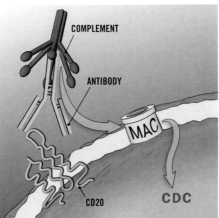

The Complement Cascade

A complement protein complex binds to the antibody and turns on the complement cascade. The end result is formation of the membrane attack complex [MAC], which creates a hole in the cell membrane that ultimately causes the cell to disintegrate. This process is known as complement-dependent cytotoxicity [CDC].

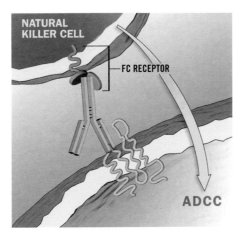

Natural Killer Cells

Antibodies that are attached to cancer cells attract natural killer [NK] cells, a type of white blood cell that circulates in the blood. A portion of the antibody called Fc binds to the Fc receptor on NK cells and initiates a process called antibody-dependent cellular cytotoxicity [ADCC] that destroys the cancer cell.

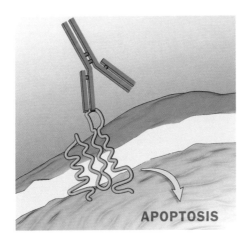

Cell Death From the Inside

Binding of antibodies to proteins on the surface of cancer cells can directly interfere with normal growth signals and activate a cell death pathway [apoptosis] inside the cell.

Vaccine Therapy

Although a number of vaccines are available to prevent cancer, vaccines that treat existing cancer are making their way through clinical testing.

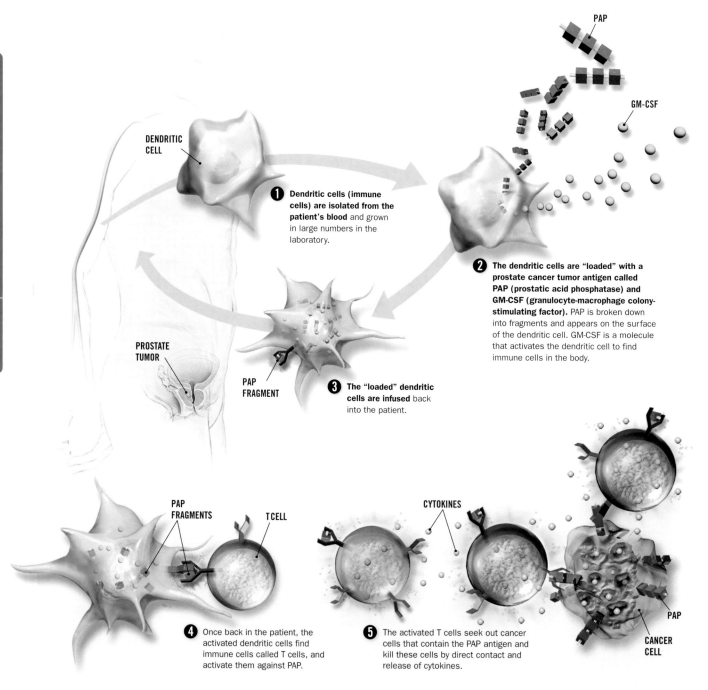

DENDRITIC CELL

PAP

GM-CSF

❶ **Dendritic cells (immune cells) are isolated from the patient's blood** and grown in large numbers in the laboratory.

❷ **The dendritic cells are "loaded" with a prostate cancer tumor antigen called PAP (prostatic acid phosphatase) and GM-CSF (granulocyte-macrophage colony-stimulating factor).** PAP is broken down into fragments and appears on the surface of the dendritic cell. GM-CSF is a molecule that activates the dendritic cell to find immune cells in the body.

PROSTATE TUMOR

PAP FRAGMENT

❸ **The "loaded" dendritic cells are infused** back into the patient.

PAP FRAGMENTS

T CELL

CYTOKINES

PAP

CANCER CELL

❹ Once back in the patient, the activated dendritic cells find immune cells called T cells, and activate them against PAP.

❺ The activated T cells seek out cancer cells that contain the PAP antigen and kill these cells by direct contact and release of cytokines.

ILLUSTRATION BY PAM CURRY

Kidney Cancer Treatments

In recent years, the arsenal of kidney cancer drugs has grown to include immunotherapy, mTOR inhibitors, and angiogenesis inhibitors.

1 Immunotherapy
Triggers the body's natural immune response to fight cancer

Ⓐ Stimulatory cytokines activate and boost the production of cytotoxic T cells

T CELL

STIMULATORY CYTOKINE

CANCER CELLS

Ⓑ Cytotoxic T cells seek out and destroy the cancer

CYTOTOXIC T CELL

2 mTOR Inhibitors
Turns off the signals that tell the cancer cell and blood vessel cells to grow

mTOR INHIBITOR

GROWTH FACTORS BIND TO RECEPTORS

CANCER CELL

SIGNALING PATHWAYS

mTOR

HIF-1

Proliferation

Angiogenesis

Ⓐ The protein mTOR plays a key role in signaling the cancer cell to grow and survive.

Ⓑ mTOR inhibitors block the mTOR pathway and prevent cancer growth.

3 Angiogenesis Inhibitors
Starves the tumor by cutting off its blood supply

Ⓐ Vascular endothelial growth factor [VEGF] is a protein produced by the tumor

VEGF

VEGF BINDS TO ITS RECEPTOR

CANCER CELLS

ANGIOGENESIS INHIBITOR

Ⓑ The binding of VEGF to its receptor stimulates the formation of new blood vessels that supply the tumor with nutrients and oxygen

ANGIOGENESIS INHIBITOR BINDS TO VEGF

Ⓒ Some angiogenesis inhibitors work by blocking the growth signal from inside the cell by binding to the tyrosine kinase portion of the VEGF receptor

Ⓓ Other angiogenesis inhibitors work by attaching to VEGF and preventing the protein from binding to its receptor

GROWTH SIGNAL

ANGIOGENESIS INHIBITOR

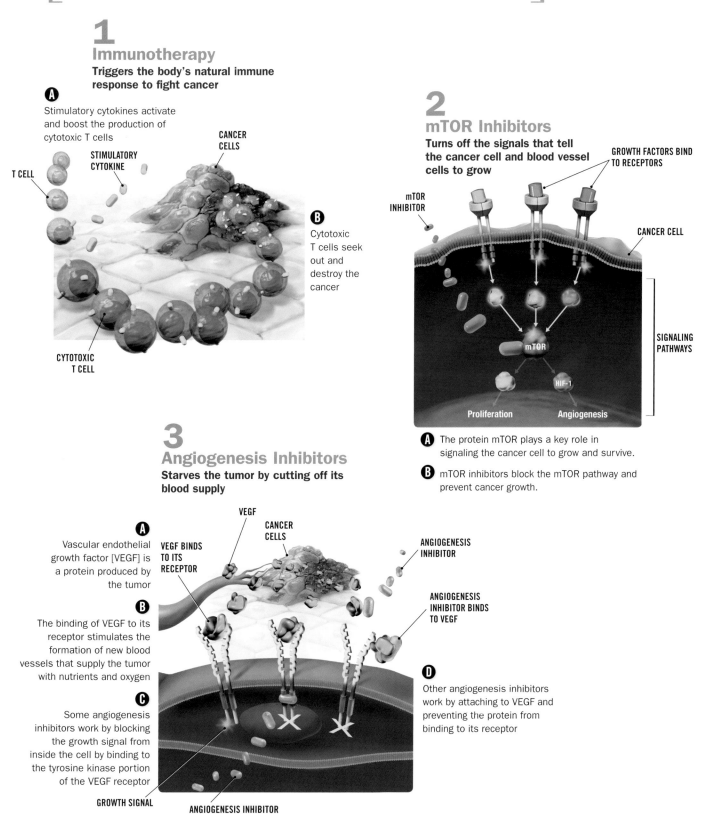

Targeting KRAS

Certain drugs target different pathways depending on the tumor cell's biology. Experimental drugs attack cancer by blocking alternate growth pathways.

Normal KRAS >

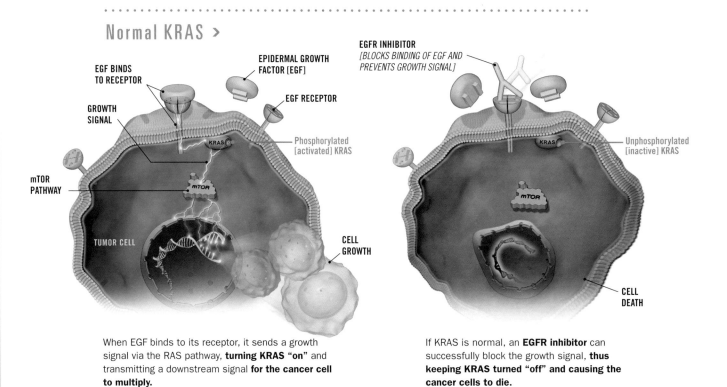

EGF BINDS TO RECEPTOR

EPIDERMAL GROWTH FACTOR [EGF]

GROWTH SIGNAL

EGF RECEPTOR

Phosphorylated [activated] KRAS

mTOR PATHWAY

TUMOR CELL

CELL GROWTH

When EGF binds to its receptor, it sends a growth signal via the RAS pathway, **turning KRAS "on"** and transmitting a downstream signal **for the cancer cell to multiply.**

EGFR INHIBITOR
[BLOCKS BINDING OF EGF AND PREVENTS GROWTH SIGNAL]

Unphosphorylated [inactive] KRAS

CELL DEATH

If KRAS is normal, an **EGFR inhibitor** can successfully block the growth signal, **thus keeping KRAS turned "off" and causing the cancer cells to die.**

Mutated KRAS >

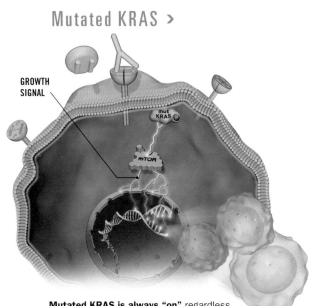

GROWTH SIGNAL

Mutated KRAS is always "on" regardless of EGFR inhibition, and **cancer cells continue to multiply.**

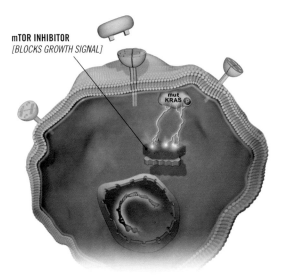

mTOR INHIBITOR
[BLOCKS GROWTH SIGNAL]

New drugs such as **mTOR inhibitors** attempt to **bypass the RAS pathway and kill the cancer** by blocking the growth signaling pathway further downstream from KRAS.

ILLUSTRATION BY ERIN MOORE

TREATMENTS

5

Immunotherapies

[Immunotherapy breaks the immune system's tolerance of cancer cells through stimulation of key immune cells and proteins.]

Normal Immune Response

Cells, such as antigen-presenting cells and lymphocytes [white blood cells], regulate the immune response when "foreign" pathogens are found. ›

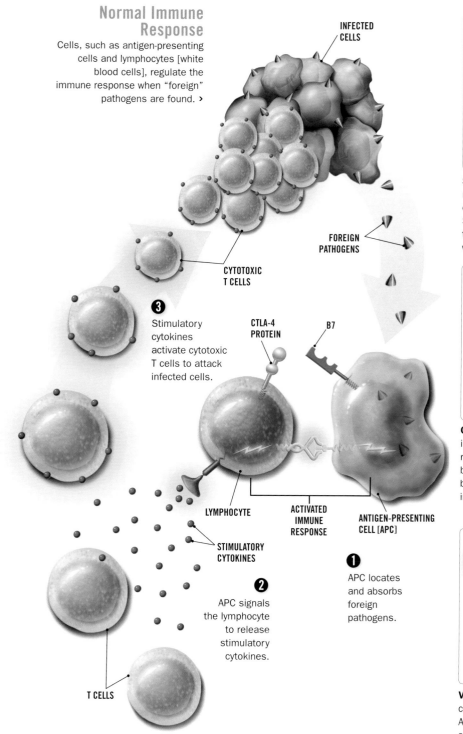

INFECTED CELLS

FOREIGN PATHOGENS

CYTOTOXIC T CELLS

❸ Stimulatory cytokines activate cytotoxic T cells to attack infected cells.

CTLA-4 PROTEIN

B7

LYMPHOCYTE

ACTIVATED IMMUNE RESPONSE

ANTIGEN-PRESENTING CELL [APC]

STIMULATORY CYTOKINES

❷ APC signals the lymphocyte to release stimulatory cytokines.

❶ APC locates and absorbs foreign pathogens.

T CELLS

Immunotherapy

Below are three ways to stimulate the body's natural immune response against cancer ›

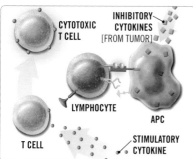

CYTOTOXIC T CELL

INHIBITORY CYTOKINES [FROM TUMOR]

LYMPHOCYTE

APC

T CELL

STIMULATORY CYTOKINE

Stimulatory cytokines: Cancer cells evade the body's natural immune response by releasing inhibitory cytokines that suppress the immune system. Stimulatory cytokines are used as therapy to override the inhibitory cytokines and activate cytotoxic T cells, which seek out and destroy the tumor.

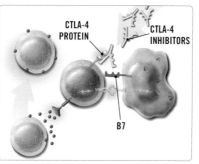

CTLA-4 PROTEIN

CTLA-4 INHIBITORS

B7

CTLA-4 Inhibitors: CTLA-4 is a protein that normally interacts with B7 on the APC to stop the immune response. CTLA-4 inhibitors are antibodies that block the binding of CTLA-4 to B7, causing the body's natural defenses to stay elevated and the immune system to continue attacking tumor cells.

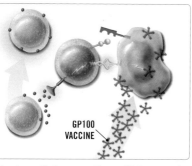

GP100 VACCINE

Vaccines: By incorporating gp100, a protein commonly found on melanoma cells, into the APC, the vaccine stimulates an immune response specifically against cancer cells that express gp100.

CURE's Illustrated Guide to Cancer

Chapter 6

Side Effects

CANCER TREATMENTS can cause side effects. Surgery may result in pain, bruising, or infection. Chemotherapy can damage healthy tissue, triggering side effects such as neuropathy, mouth sores, nausea, vomiting, and weight changes. Radiation therapy can cause rash or hair loss in the treated area, fatigue, and low blood cell counts. Most side effects fade after treatment ends and cells can repair themselves. Other side effects persist for months or years after treatment. Long-term effects may start during treatment and endure for some time after treatment has ended. For example, neuropathy may start during chemotherapy but diminish or disappear as time passes. Late effects are side effects that appear months or years after treatment is completed. Examples of late effects from treatment are heart damage and secondary cancers.

Lymphedema

Surgery or radiation on the lymph nodes may result in lymphedema, a disruption in the flow of lymph fluid that causes swelling.

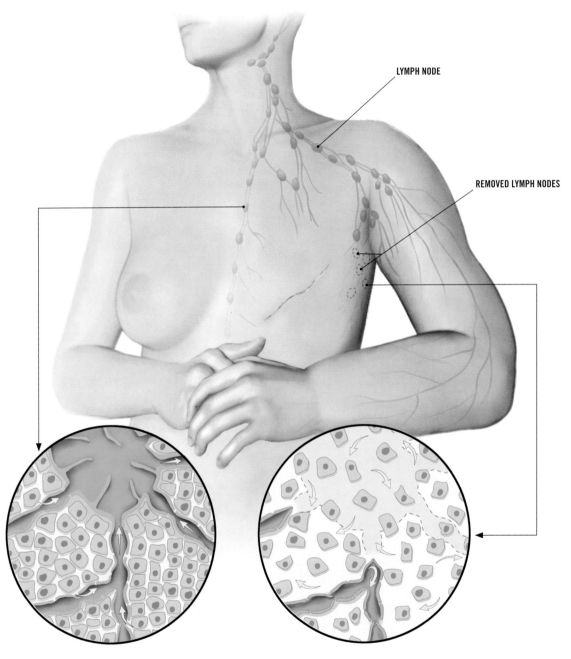

LYMPH NODE

REMOVED LYMPH NODES

Lymph nodes help maintain the body's fluid balance, filter out waste products, and defend the body against threats, such as bacteria.

The normal flow of **lymphatic fluid** is disrupted when lymph nodes are removed or destroyed. Injury, infection, or overuse can lead to a backup of fluid that causes swelling of the affected area.

ILLUSTRATION BY PAM CURRY

Heart Damage

Some cancer treatments can damage the heart in different locations and in a variety of ways.

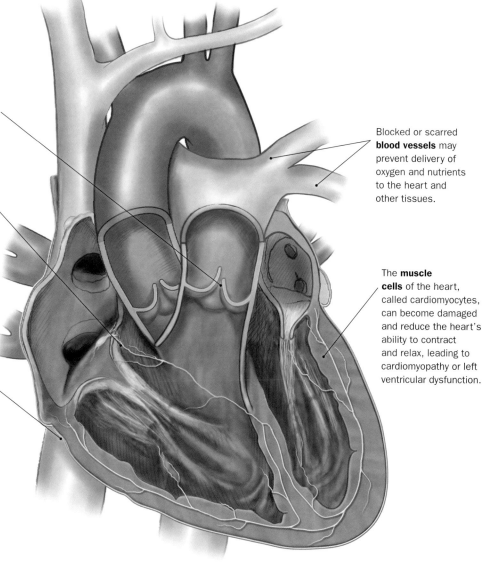

In some cases, the heart's **valves** may become stiff or leaky, reducing blood flow.

The heart's **electrical system** may become damaged, causing irregular heartbeats or arrhythmias.

Some treatments can affect the **pericardium,** the thin sac of tissue that surrounds the heart, causing it to become inflamed or scarred.

Blocked or scarred **blood vessels** may prevent delivery of oxygen and nutrients to the heart and other tissues.

The **muscle cells** of the heart, called cardiomyocytes, can become damaged and reduce the heart's ability to contract and relax, leading to cardiomyopathy or left ventricular dysfunction.

Weight Loss or Gain

Signals to the brain from the stomach intiate hunger, while serotonin released from the brain signals a feeling of fullness. Certain drugs exist that effect weight loss or gain.

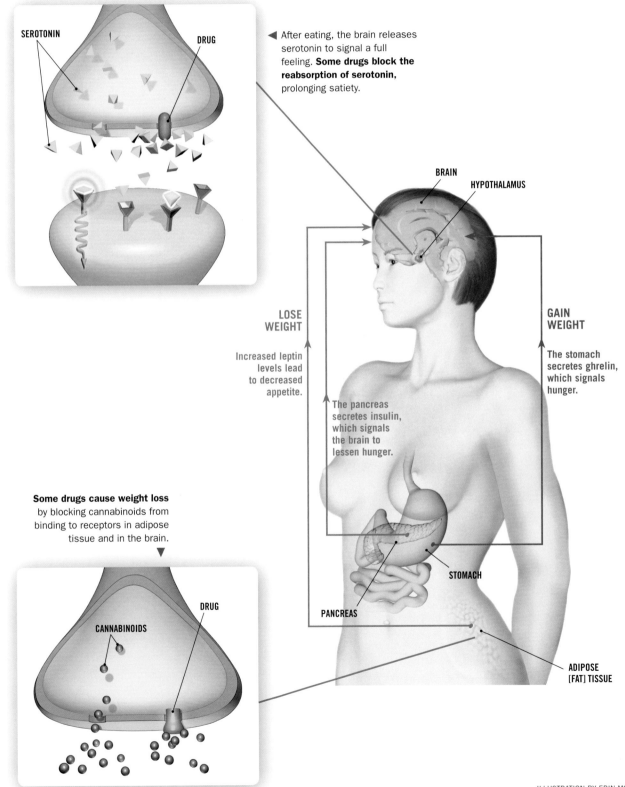

SEROTONIN

DRUG

◄ After eating, the brain releases serotonin to signal a full feeling. **Some drugs block the reabsorption of serotonin,** prolonging satiety.

BRAIN

HYPOTHALAMUS

LOSE WEIGHT

Increased leptin levels lead to decreased appetite.

GAIN WEIGHT

The stomach secretes ghrelin, which signals hunger.

The pancreas secretes insulin, which signals the brain to lessen hunger.

Some drugs cause weight loss by blocking cannabinoids from binding to receptors in adipose tissue and in the brain.

DRUG

CANNABINOIDS

STOMACH

PANCREAS

ADIPOSE [FAT] TISSUE

Rash

Epidermal growth factor receptor (EGFR) inhibitors are targeted therapies that may cause mild to severe rash.

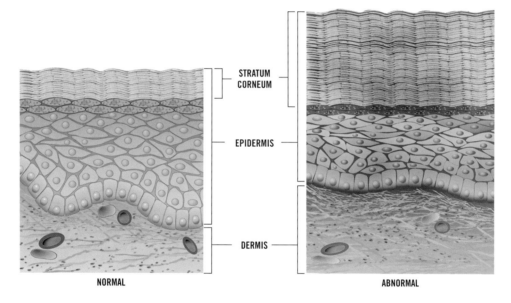

STRATUM CORNEUM

EPIDERMIS

DERMIS

NORMAL

ABNORMAL

EGFR is normally expressed in keratinocytes, the major cell type of the epidermis.

EGFR inhibitors interfere with the normal cellular processes of keratinocytes, which in turn stimulates a thickened stratum corneum and inflammation of the skin.

MRSA Infection

[MRSA is an antibiotic-resistant staph infection that can compromise the immune system and cause serious illness.]

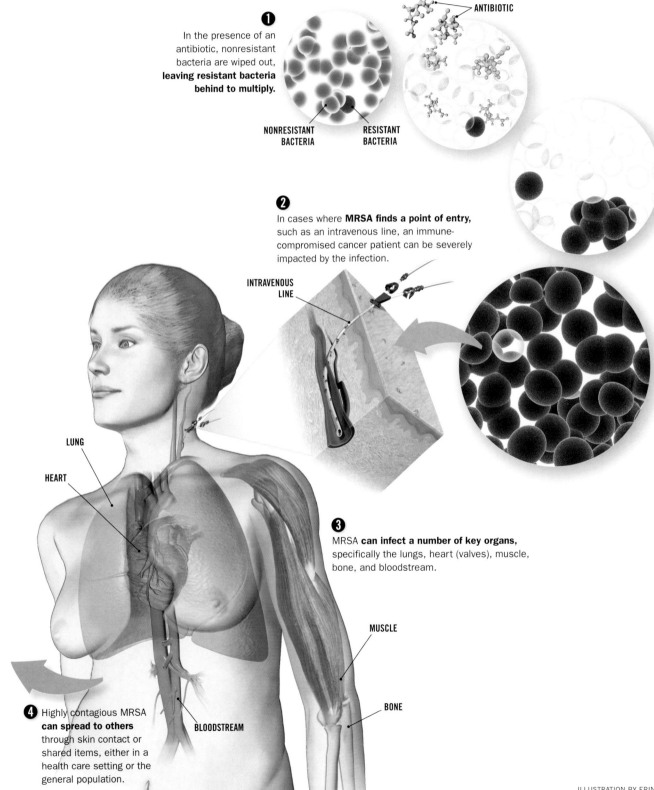

1 In the presence of an antibiotic, nonresistant bacteria are wiped out, **leaving resistant bacteria behind to multiply.**

ANTIBIOTIC

NONRESISTANT BACTERIA

RESISTANT BACTERIA

2 In cases where **MRSA finds a point of entry,** such as an intravenous line, an immune-compromised cancer patient can be severely impacted by the infection.

INTRAVENOUS LINE

LUNG

HEART

3 MRSA **can infect a number of key organs,** specifically the lungs, heart (valves), muscle, bone, and bloodstream.

MUSCLE

BONE

4 Highly contagious MRSA **can spread to others** through skin contact or shared items, either in a health care setting or the general population.

BLOODSTREAM

ILLUSTRATION BY ERIN MOORE

Bone Loss

Some treatments can cause bone tissue to break down, resulting in bones becoming weak and fragile. However, patients can take drugs to help prevent bone loss.

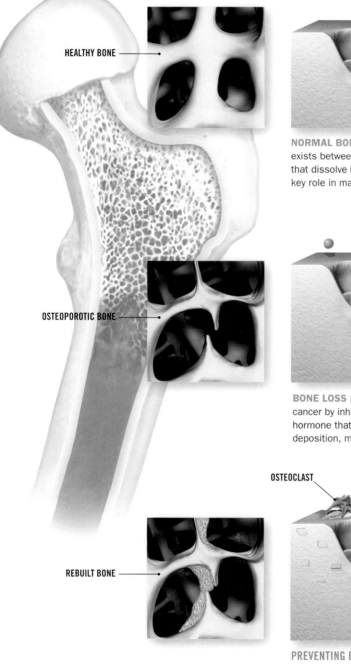

HEALTHY BONE

OSTEOPOROTIC BONE

REBUILT BONE

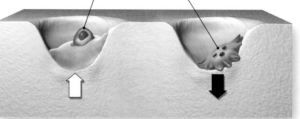

OSTEOBLAST   OSTEOCLAST

NORMAL BONE [HEALTHY BALANCE]   In normal bone, a delicate balance exists between cells that build up bone tissue, called osteoblasts, and cells that dissolve bone tissue (break it down), called osteoclasts. Estrogen plays a key role in maintaining this healthy balance and preserving bone density.

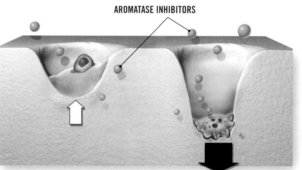

AROMATASE INHIBITORS

BONE LOSS [UNHEALTHY BALANCE]   Aromatase inhibitors treat breast cancer by inhibiting estrogen production, which, in turn, alters the amount of hormone that reaches bone cells. Without estrogen, bone loss outpaces bone deposition, making the bone porous and susceptible to fracture.

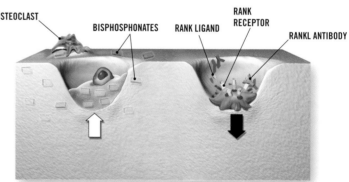

OSTEOCLAST   BISPHOSPHONATES   RANK LIGAND   RANK RECEPTOR   RANKL ANTIBODY

PREVENTING BONE LOSS

Bisphosphonates inhibit the activity of osteoclasts, while at the same time increasing osteoblast activity by protecting the bone-building cells from dying. Although bisphosphonates also increase bone mineral density by incorporating themselves into the bone matrix, the quality of the bone may remain low.

RANK ligand (RANKL), a protein that tells the body to remove bone, is an important component of the normal bone matrix. Typically, RANKL activates osteoclasts by binding to the RANK receptor. Antibodies that bind RANKL can prevent this activation process.

ILLUSTRATION BY ERIN MOORE

Pain

[
Nearly 90 percent of patients experience cancer-related pain during and/or after treatment.
Pain can often be relieved with its own array of treatment strategies.
]

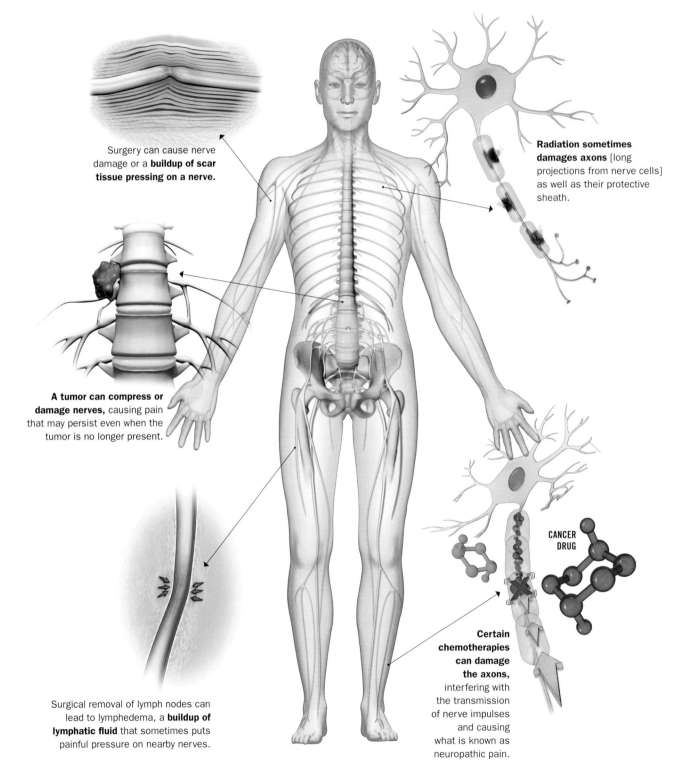

SIDE EFFECTS

6

Surgery can cause nerve damage or a **buildup of scar tissue pressing on a nerve.**

Radiation sometimes damages axons [long projections from nerve cells] as well as their protective sheath.

A tumor can compress or damage nerves, causing pain that may persist even when the tumor is no longer present.

CANCER DRUG

Certain chemotherapies can damage the axons, interfering with the transmission of nerve impulses and causing what is known as neuropathic pain.

Surgical removal of lymph nodes can lead to lymphedema, a **buildup of lymphatic fluid** that sometimes puts painful pressure on nearby nerves.

ILLUSTRATION BY ERIN MOORE

Hair Loss

Hair loss is a common side effect that can result from radiation to a treated area or from some chemotherapies.

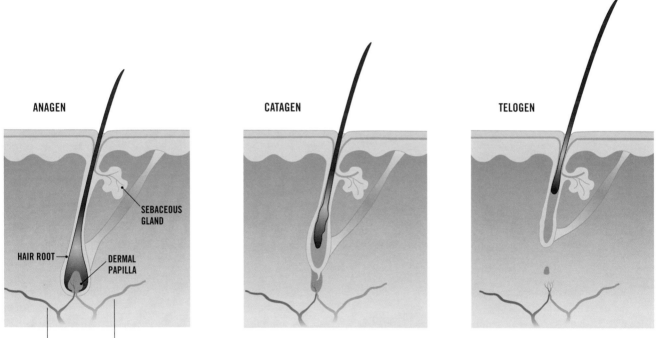

ANAGEN · CATAGEN · TELOGEN

SEBACEOUS GLAND · HAIR ROOT · DERMAL PAPILLA · CAPILLARIES

All hair follicles go through a cycle of growth (called anagen), a transitional phase (called catagen), and a terminal phase (called telogen) when the older hair falls out and a new cycle of hair growth begins. Anagen is the longest phase with up to 90 percent of follicles in that phase at any given time. The catagen phase is a transitional time when cell division slows. The telogen phase, the resting phase, is the point of hair loss. Chemotherapy affects the rapidly dividing cells in the bulb surrounding the dermal papilla, which is at the base of the hair follicle, causing hair loss. Patients who receive radiation to parts of the body where there is hair growth may lose hair in that area. Most patients will have their hair grow back once chemotherapy or radiation is completed.

Nausea & Vomiting

Many anti-nausea drugs, called antiemetics, exist to help patients with the nausea and vomiting that can accompany some treatments.

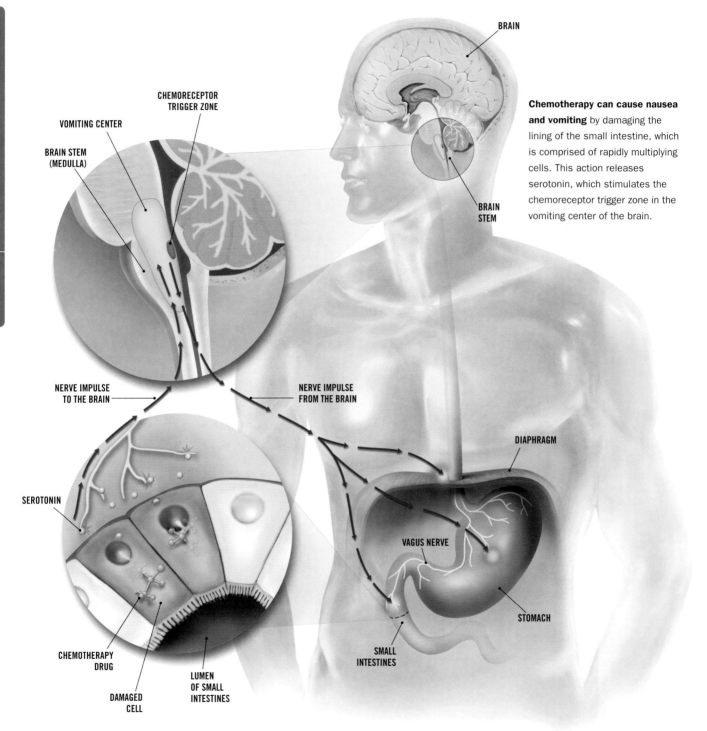

BRAIN

Chemotherapy can cause nausea and vomiting by damaging the lining of the small intestine, which is comprised of rapidly multiplying cells. This action releases serotonin, which stimulates the chemoreceptor trigger zone in the vomiting center of the brain.

CHEMORECEPTOR TRIGGER ZONE

VOMITING CENTER

BRAIN STEM (MEDULLA)

BRAIN STEM

NERVE IMPULSE TO THE BRAIN

NERVE IMPULSE FROM THE BRAIN

DIAPHRAGM

SEROTONIN

VAGUS NERVE

STOMACH

CHEMOTHERAPY DRUG

DAMAGED CELL

LUMEN OF SMALL INTESTINES

SMALL INTESTINES

ILLUSTRATION BY PAM CURRY

Neutropenia

Chemotherapy or radiation can destroy white blood cells, called neutrophils, which can result in neutropenia, making a patient more prone to infection.

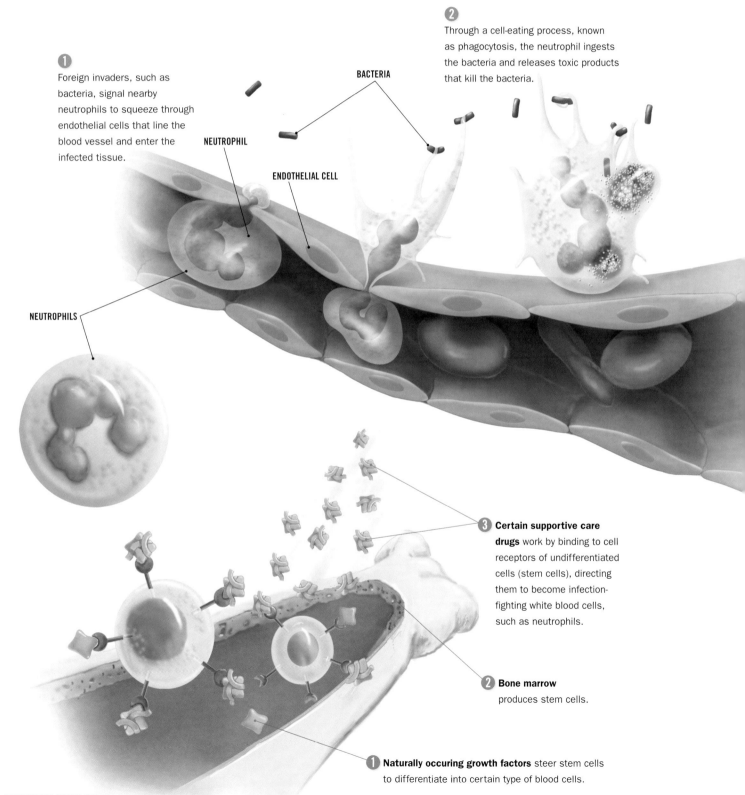

❶ Foreign invaders, such as bacteria, signal nearby neutrophils to squeeze through endothelial cells that line the blood vessel and enter the infected tissue.

❷ Through a cell-eating process, known as phagocytosis, the neutrophil ingests the bacteria and releases toxic products that kill the bacteria.

BACTERIA

NEUTROPHIL

ENDOTHELIAL CELL

NEUTROPHILS

❸ Certain supportive care drugs work by binding to cell receptors of undifferentiated cells (stem cells), directing them to become infection-fighting white blood cells, such as neutrophils.

❷ Bone marrow produces stem cells.

❶ Naturally occuring growth factors steer stem cells to differentiate into certain type of blood cells.

Peripheral Neuropathy

Peripheral neuropathy results from damage to the nervous system and may cause pain, numbness, tingling, or loss of sensation.

Neuropathy can be caused by radiation to the nerves or by a tumor close to the nerves. However, more commonly, neuropathy is caused by certain chemotherapies that damage the nerves or their environment. Nerves run up and down the body from the spine to the toes. Some patients describe the loss of sensations caused by neuropathy as similar to the feeling of wearing a stocking or glove.

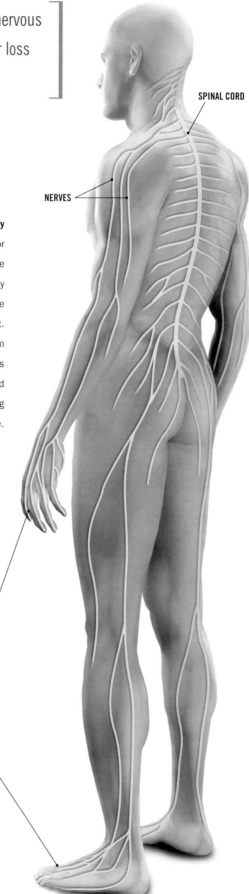

SPINAL CORD

NERVES

STOCKING OR GLOVE
DISTRIBUTION

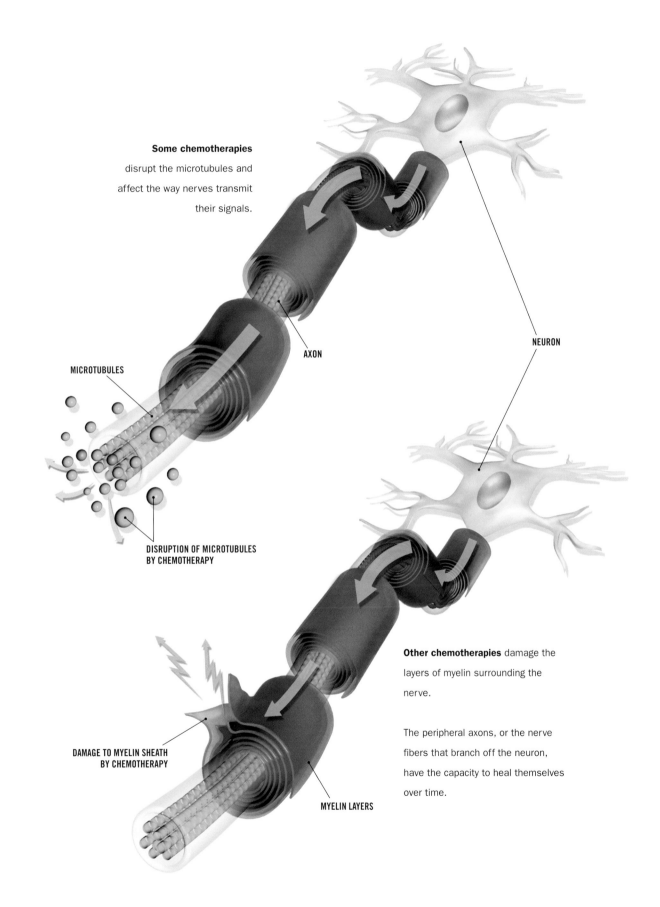

Some chemotherapies disrupt the microtubules and affect the way nerves transmit their signals.

MICROTUBULES

DISRUPTION OF MICROTUBULES BY CHEMOTHERAPY

AXON

NEURON

Other chemotherapies damage the layers of myelin surrounding the nerve.

The peripheral axons, or the nerve fibers that branch off the neuron, have the capacity to heal themselves over time.

DAMAGE TO MYELIN SHEATH BY CHEMOTHERAPY

MYELIN LAYERS

Index

At Genentech BioOncology, we're leading the fight against cancer with innovative science and fundamentally transforming the way cancer is treated. Our commitment to this goal has enabled us to make significant contributions to the understanding of cancer and to translate this understanding into targeted, biologic-based therapies.

BIO**ONCOLOGY**™

Genentech
A Member of the Roche Group